Englisch komplett beherrschen

36 Themen zur Sprachbeherrschung

Jenny Smith

Bitte besuchen Sie meine Website und abonnieren Sie meinen Newsletter für kostenlose Lernmaterialien und Informationen zu meinen anderen Büchern.

Holen Sie sich noch heute Ihren **kostenlosen** Hörverstehens-Download

englishfluencytoday.com/de

Herausgegeben von Fluency Today.

CONTENTS

Wie man ein flüssiger Englischsprecher wird

Dieses Buch ist für Englischlerner auf mittlerem Niveau geeignet.

Es gibt viele Dinge, die einen exzellenten Englischsprecher ausmachen, doch eine der Haupteigenschaften ist, dass er mit Leichtigkeit über eine Vielzahl von unterschiedlichen Themen sprechen kann. Viele Schüler auf mittlerem Niveau können über einige Themen ziemlich gut sprechen, können aber absolut nicht mithalten, wenn jemand über ein unbekanntes Thema spricht. Dieses Buch hilft Ihnen, Ihr Vokabular in 36 sehr nützlichen und häufigen Themenbereichen aufzubauen.

5 Wege, durch die Ihnen dieses Buch zum fließenden Englischssprechen verhilft

Eins) Dieses Buch deckt **36 Themenbereiche ab**, über die am häufigsten gesprochen wird. Meistern Sie diese und Sie befinden sich auf dem besten Weg, zum fließenden Englischsprechen.

Zwei) Wenn Sie sich nur über ein paar limitierte Themen unterhalten können, lernen Sie **nicht**, fließend zu sprechen. Dieses Buch hilft Ihnen dabei, diese Grenzen zu durchbrechen.

Drei) Dieses Buch bietet mehr als **600 neue Wörter und Phrasen**, die im Kontext vorgestellt werden (Kurzgeschichten oder Artikel). Dadurch macht es Spaß und veranschaulicht außerdem auf einfache Art, wie die Wörter tatsächlich verwendet werden.

Vier) Jedes neue Wort oder jede Phrase wird in einfacher englischer Sprache erklärt. Dies hilft Ihnen dabei, sich daran zu gewöhnen, auf

Englisch zu denken, anstatt ständig aus Ihrer eigenen Sprache zu übersetzen.

Fünf) Es gibt Beispielsätze für jedes neue Wort und jede Phrase. Das hilft Ihnen bei der Beherrschung, sowohl der Bedeutung als auch der Verwendung des Wortes.

Wenn Ihnen dieses Buch gefällt, hinterlassen Sie bitte eine Bewertung und sehen Sie sich auch mein anderes sehr beliebtes Buch an: 500 Wirklich Nützliche Englische Sätze.

Also, fangen wir an...

CRIME

PART ONE

The Police

Me and my partner had been working on the case for about two months. We were part of a larger sting operation to take down Henry Deacon, one of the most notorious crime bosses in town. He'd been picked up before for petty crime such as selling black-market goods but nothing ever really stuck. The evidence was either found to be inadmissible in court or the jury members would be intimidated or bought off, so he'd always walk.

Vocabulary and Phrases:

A case: Here this word means when the police investigate a crime. An investigation.

Example: *The murder case took two years to investigate.*

A sting/sting operation: This is sometimes called a 'police sting' and is a complicated operation to catch criminals.

Example: *The police sting took over a year but eventually closed the crime syndicate down.*

Notorious: This means 'famous' for doing something bad (or sometimes unorthodox).

Example: *You could say that Bonnie and Clyde are famous but 'notorious' would be a better description.*

(When someone is) picked up: 'To be picked up' has many meanings but here it refers to when someone is taken to the police station for further questioning.

Example: *The escaped convict* (someone who was in prison) *was picked up when he tried to cross the border.*

Petty crime/petty criminal: A small crime/criminal. Not a serious crime/criminal.

Example1: *Stealing from shops is considered a petty crime.*

Example 2: *He was known as a bit of a petty criminal so everyone was shocked when he robbed a bank.*

The black-market: This is when things are sold 'unofficially'. So they are not through formal channels and shops. They are untaxed.

Example: *Black-market cigarettes account for 30% of all cigarettes sold in the UK.*

When something doesn't stick: Again this has many meanings but in this context it means when the evidence against a criminal is not enough to convict them. So the police try to connect someone to a crime but it doesn't 'stick to them'.

Example: *The DNA evidence was inconclusive so the charge didn't stick.*

To be inadmissible in court: This is evidence that cannot be used in court. For some reason the evidence has become useless.

Example: *The witness was drunk when he saw the crime so his evidence is inadmissible.*

To intimidate (someone)/to be intimidated (by someone): To act in a threatening way towards someone. To feel threatened by someone. This is used for both physical and psychological intimidation.

Example 1: *He was always intimidating his wife.*

Example 2: *His wife was intimidated by him.*

To buy someone off/To be bought off: This is when someone is bribed to do something. To be paid by a criminal to ignore evidence etc.

Example 1: *The criminal bought the policeman off.*

Example 2: *The criminals in that town can do whatever they want because the whole police force has been bought off.*

(When a criminal) **walks:** This is when someone is definitely guilty but for some reason is not convicted of the crime.

Example: *Even though his alibi was obviously fake it meant that he was able to walk.*

Part Two

We'd been sitting outside of his house on a stakeout for the past week. He had not left once, when suddenly at around 3am we spotted him. He got into his car and started driving towards the western part of town. We tailed him at a distance for about a mile when he turned onto the highway. We were pretty confident that he hadn't noticed us so we maintained our distance and followed him to an abandoned warehouse. We were far away from him and we had to turn off our lights, but we could just about make-out what was happening. It seemed that it was some sort of a buy. Although it was dark, we identified the other person as a known drug importer. We rang our commanding officer but he ordered us to stand down and not to bust them as there were only two of us and it would be too risky without back-up. Even though we disagreed, that is the chain of command and we had to respect it.

Vocabulary and Phrases:

A stakeout: When the police wait outside someone's house and watch them. When the police secretly watch someone who they think may commit (has committed) a crime.

Example: The two police officers were on a stake-out watching the suspected criminal.

To tail someone: This is when someone (usually the police) follows someone else (usually a suspect) without them knowing about it.

Example: *The criminal made sure that he lost the tail before he tried to leave the country.*

To (be able to) make (something) out : This is when you cannot see something clearly but you can just about identify what it is. Note: This is not exactly a 'police show' word, but it is useful.

Example: *My daughter's drawing is a bit messy but I can just about make out that it's of a dog.*

A buy: This is often used to describe when criminals meet in secret to exchange money for (illegal) goods.

Example: *The drugs buy was caught on camera by a tourist filming on their smart phone.*

A known (criminal): This is a criminal that the police know about. The police have records/details about this criminal. This person has had past problems with the law.

Example: *He was a known criminal so the police had his finger prints on record.*

To stand down : Here it means when a police officer or solider does not attack but instead retreats.

Example: *The police man was ordered to stand down when it appeared that they were about to raid the wrong house.*

To bust (someone) for (something)/ to make a bust: This is when the police catch and charge a criminal for something. This is usually called '**an arrest**' or '**to arrest someone**'.

Example 1: *The criminal was eventually busted for drug smuggling.*

Example 2: *The criminal was eventually arrested for drug smuggling.*

Back-up: Here it means additional police officers called to assist in a difficult situation.

Example: *As soon as she realised that he had a gun, she called for back-up.*

The chain of command: In both the police and the military they have what is known as 'the chain of command'. This describes when orders are given by the superiors and those below *must* follow them.

Example: *The chain of command means that the commander is held responsible for the mess even though it wasn't directly his fault.*

PART THREE

The orders came through that we were to ignore the other suspect and resume our tail on Henry Deacon. We were then supposed to stop and search his car. We were able to tail him for about half a mile and then he must of made us as he suddenly swerved off of the main road and then tore off down a smaller road. We tried to pursue him but he managed to shake us. We doubled back and called in a description of his car. He was eventually spotted about two miles from our destination so we raced after him. We eventually caught up with him and pulled him over.

Vocabulary and Phrases:

A suspect: This is someone the police think may have committed a crime.

Example: *The main suspect suddenly tried to leave the country so the police arrested them.*

To be made: In this case it is when a the suspect realises that they are being tailed by the police and then tries to escape.

Example: *Even though the police were careful not to get too close, the suspect made them easily, and was able to lose them.*

To swerve: To turn very sharply (sometimes not on purpose). **To swerve off (onto another road):** This is when you dangerously turn onto another road. Note: This is not a 'police show' word but it is useful.

Example 1: *The car in front of me was swerving all around the place. I think the driver was drunk.*

Example 2: *The car swerved onto the smaller road.*

To tear off : To suddenly accelerate/To run off/To suddenly leave. Note: This is not a 'police show' word but it is useful.

Example: *He tore off as soon as heard the news.*

To pursue (someone): To follow (someone).

Example: *The policeman pursued the suspect on foot.*

To shake (a tail): This is when a suspect manages to lose/escape from the police who are following them.

Example: *The suspect managed to shake the police tail pretty easily.*

To double back: This is when you return the way that you came. It is sometimes used when you are lost or the purpose for going a certain direction no longer exists. Note: This is not a 'police show' word but it is useful.

Example: *We suddenly got caught in a thunder storm so we decided to double back and return home.*

To call (something) in: This is when police officers ring the police station with details or updates.

Example: *After the shooting the policeman called it in immediately.*

To spot someone/ to be spotted: To see someone from a distance. To see someone doing something.

Example 1: *I spotted him stealing sweets from a shop.*

Example 2: *He was spotted stealing sweets from a shop.*

PART FOUR

We had no idea whether Deacon was armed or not so we approached his vehicle with extreme caution. He was sitting there vey calmly but refused to get out of the car. Eventually we had to force him to get out of the car. When we searched the car we discovered a bag of money and a gun so we read him his rights and took him down to the station. We then booked him for possession of an illegal weapon.

Vocabulary and Phrases:

To be armed: To have a gun or a weapon.

Example: *Police officers in America are all armed.*

To approach with caution: This is when you should be careful when getting close to someone because they may be dangerous.

Example: *The policeman approached the suspect with caution because he thought that he might have a gun.*

To read someone their rights: When the police arrest someone they must inform them of their rights. For example 'you have the right to remain silent' etc. This is called 'reading someone their rights'.

Example: *The police officer read the suspect his rights and then took him to the police station.*

To book someone for a crime: To arrest someone for something and then enter their details in to a formal police record.

Example: *He was booked for drunk driving.*

PART FIVE

The Suspect

My name is Henry Deacon and I am a hard working law abiding businessman. For some reason the cops have had it in for me since I was young. I admit that I have had a few brushes with the law when I was younger and was even banged up for a while but I while I was inside I saw the error of my ways and turned over a new leaf. Since then I've been on the straight and narrow, and haven't so much as got a parking ticket. Nether-the-less the pigs have been hassling me ever since.

Vocabulary and Phrases:

To have it in for someone: This is when you dislike someone for no reason and you try to cause trouble for them. Note: This is not a 'police show' word, but it is useful.

Example: *That teacher always had it in for me, I think that's why I always hated school.*

A law abiding (person): Someone who obeys (follows the rules of) the law.

Example: *She was a law abiding citizen until one day she just went crazy and tried to rob a bank.*

To have a brush with the law: This is when you have had a 'little' trouble with the police. It has the feeling of not being that serious.

Example: *That area is so rough that most of the young men there have had brushes with the law.*

To be banged up: This is slang for being in prison.

Example: *He was banged up for murder.*

To be inside: In this case it refers to being in prison.

Example: *He studied law while he was inside and eventually defended himself in court.*

To see the error of one's ways: To realise that you have done something wrong. To realise that you are on the wrong path in life and to try and change it.

Example: *He was so selfish when he was younger. But he soon saw the error of his ways after he had a child and had to be responsible for someone else.*

To turn over a new leaf: This is when you try to change your life. To try to change your character or your life.

Example: *He was caught cheating at school and was thrown out. But he assures me that he has turned over a new leaf and that he will never do that again.*

To be on the straight and narrow: This is used when someone used to do illegal things but now never breaks the law.

Example: *He's been on the straight and narrow ever since he almost went to jail. He realized at that point that he needed to sort his life out.*

Part Six

I had been pretty ill for about a week so I hadn't left my house. I'd noticed that my house was being watched but it had happened so many times before that I thought nothing of it. Anyway I was starting to feel better so I thought that I'd take a drive. I drove around for a while a then took a walk. On my way home I was stopped by the police. It was then that they <u>planted</u> the gun and the money. They said that they'd <u>caught me red handed</u> but really they were just trying to <u>frame me</u> for a <u>crime</u> I didn't <u>commit</u>.

<u>Vocabulary and Phrases:</u>

To plant evidence: This is when the police/or someone places fake evidence at the scene to make it look like someone has done something against the law.

Example: *At first the police thought that it was suicide but then they noticed that the suicide note had been planted there, so they decided that it must have been murder.*

To catch someone (doing something) red handed: This means that the person was caught while in the act of doing something bad.

Example: *She caught her husband red handed with another woman.*

To frame someone for a crime: This is when someone tries to make it look like someone else has committed a crime even if they haven't. To make someone look guilty for something they didn't do.

Example: *He always said that he was framed but the police found his fingerprints on the murder weapon.*

To commit a crime: To do a crime. 'Commit' is the verb used with a lot of crimes. For example, to commit murder/suicide.

Example: *He committed his first crime when he was still in high school.*

Part Seven

At the station.

When we got him back to the station he started protesting his innocence and shouting that he'd never seen the gun before in his life. We ran the gun through the computer and it was connected to two unsolved murders. This was excellent news for us, not only did we have him bang to rights on the drug deal we could also pin two murders on him as well. After years of getting off scot free we now had him and we intended to throw the book at him. We were going to make sure that he would go down for this.

Vocabulary and Phrases:

To protest one's innocence: To insist with lots of passion that you are innocent.

Example: *Even though we caught him red handed he was still protesting his innocence to the end.*

To have someone bang to rights (UK only. Very rarely used): To have 100% solid evidence against someone.

Example: *The police had him bang to rights on the murder charge.*

To get off scot free: To not get punished even though you did something bad. To not be convicted (found guilty in court) even if you committed a crime.

Example: *When we were kids my brother always got off scot free but I was always punished.*

To pin a crime on someone: This is when the police connect someone with a certain crime. It can be used in the context when the person is actually guilty and when the person is innocent.

Example 1: *The police found his fingerprints on the weapon so were able to pin the murder on him.*

Example 2: *The police tried to pin the murder on him even though he had an alibi.*

To throw the book at someone: To try and punish someone (through the legal system) as much as possible.

Example: *Because the child eventually died they threw the book at the drunk driver that caused it.*

To go down for something: To go to prison. To be sent to prison.

Example: *He went down for 10 years after admitting to manslaughter.*

More Useful Words:

An alibi: This is when someone has a witness to them being somewhere else at a particular time, which proves that they couldn't have committed the crime.

An airtight alibi: This is when the alibi is 100% certain.

A snitch (US and UK)/a grass (UK only): This is a criminal who gives information to the police about other criminals in order to go free or to benefit in some way. So they betray other criminals.

A police informant: This is a person (usually involved in the criminal world) who sells information to the police. The slang term for them is (police) snitches (see above).

Under-cover police: This is a police officer that is pretending to be a criminal in order to catch real criminals.

Pigs (US/UK)/filth (UK only)/fuzz (UK only): These are all very insulting terms for the police.

Top brass (UK): The top police. Management.

Manslaughter: To kill someone by accident.

First degree murder: To plan to kill someone in advance and then actually do it.

DUI (US): Driving under the influence (of alcohol). This is the name of the crime. So the police charge drink drivers with a 'DUI'.

Ma'am: This is a word used when addressing a senior person who is female. It is often used in UK police shows. It is also used regularly in the US when respectfully addressing women.

Guv: This word is used in UK police shows when police officers are addressing their boss. It's a bit like 'sir' or 'madam'. It stands for **gov**ernor.

Extra Practice

There are a lot of different police shows and films that you could watch, and of course you should watch as many as possible. But here are some for you to consider. Please be careful and research them first as many are **very violent,** intended for adults and feature bad language.

Easier:

The Bill: This is a long running UK police show. The stories are quite simple and there isn't too much slang.

Southland: Each episode is a new story. It follows different types of police officers in Los Angeles. The stories are quite simple and there isn't too much slang.

Columbo: This is quite old but is still good. It follows the work of one detective. Each episode is a new story.

More difficult:

CSI: This show concentrates on a forensic department within the police force. The stories are quite simple but there is a lot of 'technical' language. There are lots of different series set in different US cities. For example CSI Miami and CSI New York.

Dexter: This is a show about a serial killer that works in the Miami Police Department. One story runs for the whole season, but the language used is not that difficult.

Prime Suspect: Very famous UK police show starring Helen Mirren. Very dark and realistic.

Most difficult:

The Shield: This show is set on the streets of LA and is pretty violent. The stories are not too complicated but there is a lot of slang.

The Wire: This is by far the most difficult TV programme to understand *ever*. It features a very complicated plot with lots of different characters. There is a lot of **very** difficult slang. I am a native English speaker and it took me four episodes to 'get the hang of' the slang. However, it is very interesting and has five seasons so you will get a lot of practice. If you can understand this show completely it is proof that you are finally 100% fluent in English.

LAW

PART ONE

Every now and then there is a murder trial which really divides public opinion. Some people feel that the accused definitely committed the crime, while others are not that sure. One recent example was that of Joe Phillips. He was a respected local business man with lots of ties to the local community. About two years ago his business partner was shot in the back in what looked like a cold blooded murder. Mr Phillips was initially questioned by the police but denied knowing anything about it. Later that day the police discovered that a witness had seen Mr Phillips physically fighting with the victim. He was soon taken into custody for questioning. As he couldn't produce an alibi and most of the evidence pointed toward him, he was formally charged with murder.

Vocabulary and Phrases:

The accused: The person who is suspected of committing a crime. This is a term used in court.

Example: *The accused sat in silence and refused to look at the judge.*

Cold blooded murder: This is when the murder was done on purpose and not because of some emotional or self defense reason. It is similar to 'premeditated murder' which is a murder that has been carefully planned in advance.

Example: *It was decided that it was cold blooded murder and that she had done it to collect the insurance money.*

A witness: A person that saw a crime being committed. Or an alibi that saw the accused at a different place from where the crime was committed.

Example 1: *There was a witness that saw the man being robbed.*

Example 2: *The witness said that he had seen the accused in a bar at the other side of town when the murder occurred. This means that the accused could not have committed the crime.*

To be taken into custody: To be taken to the police station when they suspect you of something.

Example: *He was taken into custody when they discovered that he had bought an illegal gun.*

To be charged with (a crime): This is when the police officially say that they think that you committed the crime.

Example: *He was formally charged with fraud. The trial should start some time early next year.*

PART TWO

His lawyer immediately requested bail but it was denied as there were fears that Mr Phillips may try to skip bail. The defense* immediately started to build a case to prove his innocence. Of course the prosecution was busy trying to prove that he was guilty. From the outside it was starting to look like an open and shut case. There was a witness that placed him at the scene of the crime an hour before the murder. He was also seen fighting with the victim. He had a motive, because he would gain full control of the company and make millions of pounds if his partner was dead. The only thing that was missing was a murder weapon.

*US spelling = defense. UK spelling defence.

Vocabulary and Phrases:

Bail/to skip bail: This is money you can pay to be released from the police station after you have been charged. You will of course have to return for the court case. To 'skip bail' or 'jump bail' is when you are released on bail (or 'out on bail') and then run away.

Example 1: *Bail was set at $30000, so there was no way that he could afford it.*

Example 2: *He skipped bail, so if he gets caught he will be sent straight to jail.*

Example 3: *The police didn't think that he was dangerous so he is out on bail now.*

Innocence/Guilt: If someone didn't do the crime then they are 'innocent'. If they did do the crime then they are 'guilty'.

Example 1: *He was caught on camera doing it, so he's definitely guilty.*

Example 2: *I don't know why, maybe it's the way he speaks, I just think that he's innocent.*

The prosecution: In a criminal court this is the side (lawyers etc) that is accusing someone of doing a crime.

Example: *The prosecution brought 100's of witnesses in to prove that the defendant was guilty.*

The defense: In a criminal court the individual being accused of the crime is 'the defendant', and their team of lawyers etc are called 'the defense'.

Example: *The defense argued that the defendant was not even in the same town at the time of the murder.*

An open and shut case: This is a case where it is very clear who committed the crime.

Example: *He was found holding the murder weapon so it was a pretty open and shut case.*

A motive: A reason for committing a crime.

Example: *His motive for committing the crime was jealousy. He had discovered that his wife was having an affair.*

PART THREE

On the first day of the trial, Mr Phillips entered a plea of not guilty. The trial eventually lasted three months with around 30 people testifying for and against the accused. It seemed that he would definitely be convicted . Then suddenly it was discovered that the main witness for the prosecution had committed perjury and had not seen a fight at all. In fact it emerged that he was a long time enemy of Mr Phillips and that he had lied. Of course the case against the accused was mainly based on the witness' testimony that he'd seen a fight. Mr Phillips was eventually found not guilty by the jury and was acquitted. He later said that when the jury delivered a verdict of not guilty it was the happiest moment of his life. The witness however was immediately charged with perjury, but he is expected to appeal against it.

Vocabulary and Phrases:

A trial: This is when a criminal case is heard in the court.

Example: *The trial lasted three years and cost millions of pounds.*

To enter a plea (of guilty/not-guilty): This is when at the beginning of the trial the defendant says whether they are guilty or not. If they say 'not guilty' then the trial tries to find out if they are telling the truth or not. It is also called 'pleading guilty' or 'pleading not guilty'.

Example 1:*The defense entered a plea of not guilty.*

Example 2: *The defendant shocked the court by immediately pleading guilty.*

To testify: To give evidence in court. To say something officially in court.

Example: *He testified that he had never met the victim in his life.*

To be convicted: When it is decided by the court that you are guilty.

Example: *He was convicted of fraud and sent to prison for 6 months.*

To commit perjury: To lie in a court case.

Example: *If you commit perjury you will perhaps be sent to jail.*

The accused: This is the person who is being accused of the crime. Also known as the defendant.

Example: The accused denied committing the crime.

Testimony: This is what people officially say in a court case. For example, if a witness sees something, then they give a 'testimony' that they saw that thing. The verb is 'to testify' (see above).

Example 1: *The witness gave his testimony and then left.*

Example 2: *The witness testified that he saw the defendant at the scene of the crime.*

Jury: These are the 'everyday' people in the court that have to decide whether someone is guilty or not.

Example: *The jury only took ten minutes to decide on a not guilty verdict.*

To be acquitted: This is when the court decides that you are not guilty and that you are free to go.

Example: *There just wasn't enough evidence so she was acquitted.*

A verdict: This is the guilty or not guilty decision (often decided by the jury).

Example: *The not guilty verdict surprised everyone.*

To appeal: This is when you lose a court case and then go back to court again to have the decision reversed.

Example: *He lost the court case but is expected to appeal as soon as possible.*

Extra Practice

There are a lot of different 'Legal Shows' but here are a few to get you started.

Law and Order: This is a good one to start with as it features both the police case and the court case that follows it.

The Good Wife: This show centers around a group of lawyers and a politician who is sent to prison. It is quite easy to understand.

Rake: This is an Australian show that stars a lawyer who has a very messy personal life. There are not many 'court room' scenes. It also features lots of famous Australian actors in cameo roles.

Silk: This is a UK legal drama. It may be slightly more difficult to understand.

THE NEWS

PART ONE

Tonight there have been unconfirmed reports of outbreaks of violence in Smithville. There have been mounting tensions over the past months between the ruling party and the opposition. While there has been tension for years, clashes started to flare up after one of the shadow ministers John Jones was assassinated. Since then tensions have been running high.

Vocabulary and Phrases:

Unconfirmed reports: This is exactly what it sounds like. 'Reports or information' which has not been officially confirmed. So it may or may not be true.

Example: *There have been unconfirmed reports that the princess is pregnant.*

Outbreaks of violence: This describes when incidents of violence occur in various small events at different locations.

Example: *There were outbreaks of violence but the police managed to contain things easily.*

Mounting tensions: This is when tensions between two (or more) parties are getting worse and worse. Another common phrase is 'mounting fears' and describes when fears of 'something bad' happening are growing.

Example: *There have been mounting tensions within my family as to whether we should put our Grandmother in an old people's home or not.*

The ruling party / the opposition: The ruling party is the party that is running the government. The opposition is the party that wants to be voted in to run the government.

Example: *The opposition has accused the ruling party of incompetence.*

To clash/ clashes: This word is often used in the news and it means the same thing as 'battle' or 'confrontation'. It can refer to both physical and non-physical disagreements.

Example 1: *The police clashed with protesters throughout the night.*

Example 2: *There were clashes between local youths all night long.*

To flare up: This is when tensions/violence/disagreements occur/get worse.

Example: *Every time my whole family gets together, tensions flare up.*

Shadow (ministers) (UK English): This is a member of the non-ruling political party (often called the opposition party(see above)).

Example: *The Shadow Health Minister accused the government of putting profits in front of patient care.*

To be assassinated: To be killed for a political reason.

Example: *He was assassinated while giving a speech about public safety.*

Tensions are running high: Again this is exactly what it sounds like and describes a situation where everyone is very tense.

Example: *Ever since we heard that there would be some redundancies, tensions have been running high at my work.*

Part Two

Just before his assassination a memo was leaked where the Prime Minister dubbed Mr Jones 'a traitor' and eluded that he had links to certain radical anti-government groups. Sources close to Mr Jones claim that that those claims were completely unfounded. Mr Jones had been gaining a lot of support over the past year and was poised to become a real threat to the ruling party at the next elections.

Vocabulary and Phrases:

To leak something: This is when secret information is made public. This is always disclosed (told) against the will of the person/party involved.

Example: *It was leaked that the politician was actually involved in tax evasion.*

To be dubbed (something): To be called (a name). When an event or person is named something for a certain reason.

Example: *The uprising in Egypt was dubbed 'The Arab Spring'.*

A traitor: Someone who betrays someone else. Someone who betrays their country.

Example 1: *I can't believe my best friend is still friends with my ex-wife even after what she did to me. He is such a traitor.*

Example 2: *The spy sold secrets to the other country so is basically a traitor.*

To elude that….: This means that something was 'hinted at'. To not say something directly but 'to convey' that meaning.

Example: *Even though he never said it directly, he eluded to the fact that he was considering retirement.*

To have links/ties to (something): To have connections with something.

Example: *The new finance minister has ties to one of the biggest banks so he is probably not to be trusted.*

Sources close to (someone): A 'source' is someone who provides information about something. So a 'source close to (someone)' is a source who is in direct contact with the person the story is about.

Example: *Sources close to the pop star say that she is recovering from exhaustion but will resume her tour as soon as possible.*

Unfounded reports/allegations: This is when something is not true. Is just based on rumor and not on fact.

Example 1: *The reports of his death were completely unfounded. He is actually alive and well and living in Spain.*

Example 2: *There were some unfounded allegations of fraud but nothing really came of it.*

To be poised (to do something) (for something to happen): You are just about to do something. This thing is just about to happen.

Example 1: *I was poised to win the Gold when my knee gave out on me and I fell over.*

Example 2: *She was poised to become the next big A-list actress and then she suddenly retired without warning.*

Part Three

Since his death many people have felt that they no longer have a voice and this has sparked anger amongst some of the poorer communities. We will now go to our correspondent on the ground for an update.

Vocabulary and Phrases:

To have a voice: This is when certain groups are able to get their opinions and concerns heard by those in power. When people's views are represented by the government.

Example: *Young people often feel that they don't really have a voice when it comes to local matters.*

To spark (anger): To cause anger etc.

Example: *The politician sparked anger when he made the sexist remarks.*

(The reporter) on the ground: (The reporter) who is actually at the scene of the news story.

Example: *Our reporter on the ground has the full story.*

A correspondent: A journalist.

Example: *Our Middle Eastern correspondent has the full story now.*

EXTRA PRACTICE

There are lots of different news channels such as CNN, Sky and BBC news 24 which you should try to watch as much as possible. Also I would suggest watching BBC's Newsnight as it has extended coverage of the main stories. If you are interested in economics and finance I would suggest The Keiser Report as it is both informative and very entertaining.

News channels on Youtube.

Channel 4.

Youtube News.

New York Times.

Al Jazeera English.

Food and Cooking

This is a very short chapter about cooking. By this stage in your language learning (intermediate level) you should be familiar with most of the words connected to food and cooking. Therefore we will concentrate on words and phrases that are useful but not covered in most English guides. But before we do, please just make sure that you are familiar with the common terms listed below. If you don't recognise one, please grab a dictionary and look it up, as they are all in daily use.

Common cooking terms:

To fry, to bake, to chop, to cut, to slice, to boil, to steam, to roast, to soak, to toast, to drain, to mash, to roll, to knead, to peel. to skin, to marinade, to glaze, to sear, to season, to sprinkle, to simmer, to drizzle.

Party Food

Every year around Christmas, my friends and I have a little tradition where we take it in turns to hold a small drinks party. It's usually really fun and we get to meet new people and to catch up with each other. This year was my turn. Now, I have no problem hosting the party but to be honest I absolutely hate cooking. So I decided that I would just do finger food. I decided that rather than just cooking a few big dishes that I would knock up a load of different light bites. So I made some savory nibbles, and some assorted dips. I also made spicy fruit punch for the kids which they all slurped down in one gulp. I thought that I'd cooked enough but everyone wolfed down the food within minutes so either they were really hungry or I didn't make enough. All in all it was a pretty fun party but I'm glad that I don't have to do it again next year.

Vocabulary and Phrases:

Finger food/ light bites/ nibbles: These words all basically describe the same thing and that is small snacks.

Example 1: *I don't think people will be in the mood for a full sit down mean so let's just put out some finger food.*

Example 2: *They didn't provide much food, just some light bites.*

Example 3: *It was a pretty good wedding except there were only nibbles, not any real food.*

To knock up some food: This describes when you very quickly prepare some really simple food. Note: be careful when using this as it sounds similar to 'knock *someone* up' which means to get someone pregnant.

Example: *I don't have much energy after work so I usually just knock something very simple up, and eat that.*

A savory (dish): This is any type of food which is not sweet.

Example: *I much prefer savoury foods to sweet things.*

A dip: This is a type of sauce that you can dip crackers or celery/carrots etc into.

Example: *I love sour cream and chive dip.*

To slurp: This is when you drink very noisily.

Example: *I hate it when people slurp when they drink.*

To wolf (food) down: This is when you eat very quickly.

Example: *I was so hungry that I wolfed my dinner down in about 3 minutes.*

To gulp: This is a loud swallowing sound. In the above paragraph it is to 'swallow in one gulp' which means that you ate something quickly.

Example: *He always made a gulping sound when he drank. It was quite unattractive.*

There are hundreds of different food and cooking shows. Here are some of the more popular cooking programme presenters. Each one has lots of different shows.

Famous Cooking Show Presenters.

Jamie Oliver

Julia Child

Delia Smith

Gordon Ramsey

Cooking Channels on Youtube.

Betty's kitchen.

Food Wishes

Simple Cooking Channel

Show me the Curry

PROPERTY

PART ONE

They say that moving house is one of the most stressful things to do next to divorce and losing a loved one. I'm not sure if that is true there is certainly a lot of stuff to think and worry about when you go <u>house hunting</u>. Firstly you have to think about what type of house you want. Do you want a house that is completely finished or would you like a <u>renovation property</u>. The advantage of buying somewhere which has <u>room for improvement</u> is that you can <u>add value</u> and also <u>make your mark</u>.

<u>Vocabulary and Phrases:</u>

To go house hunting: This describes the act of searching for a property to buy or to rent.

Example: *Using the internet has made house hunting a lot easier.*

A renovation property/To renovate: 'To renovate' is when you fix a property up, so a 'renovation property' is a building which needs work done on it.

Example: *I don't have much money so I'm going to buy a renovation property and then renovate it myself.*

Room for improvement: This means that it can be improved upon.

Example: *Even though you could live in it, there is definitely room for improvement.*

To add value: This is when you make improvements on a property, which then causes its value to go up.

Example: *We made the kitchen bigger in order to have more space and to add value to the property.*

To make your mark (on something): Here this phrase means to 'put your personality onto something' and to change it. So for example if you changed the house to have a very 'modern' feel, then you have *made your mark* on it.

Example: *When I moved to my new house, I really wanted to make my mark on it so I re-did it to exactly how I like things.*

PART TWO

The next thing you need to worry about is what the area is like. Is it an up-and-coming area or more of a commuter town. Also if you have kids you have to consider whether you are in the catchment area for the best schools. Another thing is whether it has good local amenities and transport links.

Vocabulary and Phrases:

An up-and-coming area: An area which is becoming popular.

Example: *Where I grew up used to be horrible but I hear that it's quite an up-and-coming area nowadays.*

A commuter town: This is a small town near a big city where people live in but commute to work in the city.

Example: *I live in a small commuter town near London. It's ok but a bit boring as there is nothing much to do.*

A catchment area: This is the area around somewhere like a school or a hospital that is served by that institution. For example if you live inside the catchment area of ABC School you can go there. If you live outside the catchment area however, you must go to school somewhere else.

Example: *Unfortunately we live outside of the catchment area of the best school in the area so our son couldn't go there.*

Amenities: These are things like shops and local services like libraries and schools.

Example: *My new house is pretty nice but there are no real amenities in the local area so we have to drive for everything.*

Transport links: This is basically the network of busses and trains that connect a certain area to other places.

Example: *Even though there is not much work around there, the transport links are excellent so you can probably commute to work pretty easily.*

PART THREE

Now we come to the deciding factor, and that is the price. Even if the house has the wow factor and literally ticks all of the boxes it doesn't matter if you can't afford it. Because even if you like it, you won't be able to buy it. Nowadays more people than ever want to get on the property ladder so it is definitely a seller's market. This has meant that asking prices are at an all time high so first time buyers in particular have a difficult time getting started. My advice would be to avoid houses that have already been renovated and try to find a nice fixer-upper that you can do up slowly.

Vocabulary and Phrases:

The wow factor: This phrase is used about houses that are really impressive. Note: this phrase is usually only used on TV and not in everyday conversation.

Example: *That property was alright but it didn't really have the wow factor. So I think that I'll keep looking for somewhere else.*

To tick all of the boxes : This means that a property totally meets what you want. It fits all of the criteria that you set. Note: again this phrase is only ever really used on TV.

Example: *This house has three nice bedrooms, a garage and a huge garden. It really ticks all of the boxes.*

The property ladder: This describes being a property owner. If you own a house etc then you are 'on the property ladder'. If you don't, then you are not on the ladder.

Example: *I have no interest in getting onto the property ladder, I'm very happy to just rent a place.*

A seller's market: This is when the seller has the control and can ask for a high price because a lot of people want to buy from them. The opposite is of course 'a buyer's market'.

Example 1: *There are hardly any good properties around so it really is a seller's market.*

Example 2: *When the house prices dropped in the US it was a buyer's market and you could buy nice properties at a real discount.*

Asking prices: The price the seller advertises the property for.

Example: *The asking price was unrealistic so I offered him a lot less.*

A fixer-upper: This is a property that needs to be renovated, but will be nice when it is fixed.

Example: *It's a bit of a fixer-upper but the building is pretty solid so most of the work is just cosmetic.*

To do (something/somewhere) up: This means 'to fix' or to 'improve' something/somewhere.

Example: *It was a ruin when I bought it but I spent a few years doing it up and it's absolutely great now.*

There are two types of property show. The first is where the hosts take people around to find a house to buy. The second is where people renovate a property or build a new house.

House hunting.

Location Location Location: This is the most popular of these shows in the UK. The presenters help members of the public go house hunting.

Property Ladder: This is basically the same as above.

A place in the sun; home or away: This is similar to the above show but people have to look for a property both in the UK and somewhere warmer. They then decide which place they would prefer to live in.

Renovation/building.

Grand Designs: This show is very popular and features people who build their own (often unusual) houses.

ROMANCE

PART ONE

I don't know about you but it takes a lot for me to fall for someone. But with him, I would have to say that it was love at first sight. Thinking back I would probably just call it lust rather than love, but that's how I felt at the time. From the moment I laid eyes on him I fancied him. We both attended the same university and while we didn't have any of the same classes I'd always see him in the library sitting on his own studying. He never seemed to notice me but I knew immediately that I wanted to go out with him.

Vocabulary and Phrases:

To fall for (someone): To start to love someone. To fall in love with someone. To become romantically interested in someone.

Example: *Although he wasn't very handsome, because of his personality, I fell for him immediately.*

Love at first sight: When you fall in love with someone the first time you see them.

Example: *It was love at first sight for me and my wife.*

Lust/to lust after someone: To desire someone. To have sexual feelings toward someone. This is more of a physical than emotional feeling.

Example: *I think that a lot of people mistake lust for love.*

To fancy someone: To be interested in someone romantically.

Example: *I didn't really fancy her at first but once I got to know her I fell for her pretty quickly.*

To go out with (UK)/ To date (US): To be boyfriend and girlfriend. To be in a romantic relationship with someone.

Example: *We went out with each other for a few years but then ended it when he went off to work abroad.*

PART TWO

Now I have never 'pulled' anyone in my life, I even find flirting to be a bit embarrassing. But I made my mind up that if I was ever going to meet him I'd have to make the first move. I asked my friends for advice but they were all totally useless. This was because they were usually the one's getting hit on and not the other way around. Eventually I bought a book called 'How to Chat Up Boys'. It was filled with the usual stuff like cheesy pick up lines, so I decided to ignore that too.

Vocabulary and Phrases:

To pull (someone) (UK): To talk to someone and get them to go on a date with you. This is a slang term and used in very casual language.

Example: *I don't know how he does it but every time we go to a party he manages to pull.*

To flirt (with someone): To speak to someone (who you are romantically interested in) in a way that is playful and makes it clear that you are interested in them.

Example: *I'm not that good at flirting, I always say something weird and put the guy off.*

To make the first move: To be the one to make a romantic advance on the other person.

Example: *In most cultures it's the man that makes the first move.*

To hit on (someone) (US): This is when you try to flirt with someone. You try to get them to be interested in you. Note: Be careful as 'to hit' and 'to hit *on*' have completely different meanings.

Example: *I hate that bar, all the guys are constantly trying to hit on all the girls.*

To chat (someone) up (UK): To flirt with someone and try to get with them romantically.

Example: *I can never chat girls up, I never know what to say.*

Pick up lines: To 'pick someone up' is the US version of 'to pull'. So a 'pick up line' is a phrase that you use to start a conversation with someone that you are interested in romantically. The UK version is a 'chat up line'.

Example: *Probably the most common pick up line is 'do you come here often?' which to be honest is not that good of a line.*

Then one day out of the blue, he suddenly came over to my desk and asked me out on a date. I was completely shocked as I didn't think he even knew that I existed. I thought for a second about playing hard to get, as that was the advice I got from the useless book. But I thought for a second and decided to not be an idiot and to just say 'yes'. We dated for about three months and I was completely head over heels in love with him. Then slowly his attitude towards me started to change and he seemed a bit cold and distant.

Vocabulary and Phrases:

To ask someone out: To invite someone on a date.

Example: *I was so nervous when I asked her out, that I almost didn't hear her answer.*

To play hard to get: This is when you pretend that you are not interested in someone in order to trick them into being even more interested in you.

Example: *I don't really like girls that play hard to get. If they are interested they should just be straight about it.*

To be head over heels in love (with someone): To be completely 100% in love with someone.

Example: *We were head over heels in love when we first started to date, but we soon grew tired of each other after we got married!*

Part Four

Then I started to hear rumours that he had been playing the field and that he was well known for two timing girls. I confronted him but he always laughed and said that it was funny because he was the complete opposite of 'a player'. I tried to ignore the rumours and refused to believe that he would cheat on me, but at the back my mind I couldn't shake the feeling that it was true. Then one of my best friends rang me with the news that he had hooked up with another friend of hers. I went around to his house immediately to ask him if he had gotten off with this girl. When I got to his house, to my shock and horror, I saw him through the window snogging the other girl.

Vocabulary and Phrases:

To play the field: To date lots of people (sometimes at the same time).

Example: *I was never the one to play the field when I was younger.*

To two time (someone)/ a two timing…..: This is when you have two partners and they don't know about it. To cheat on someone.

Example 1: *I had no idea that she was actually two timing me the whole time we were going out with each other.*

Example 2: *My ex-husband was a complete two timing liar.*

A player (US): Someone (usually a man) who has lots of partners and is not that serious about relationships.

Example: *I would stay away from him if I were you, he's a bit of a player.*

To cheat on (someone): To be unfaithful to someone. To date/sleep with someone else even though you have a regular partner.

Example: *It turned out that she was cheating on her boyfriend for the past few months.*

To hook up (with someone): This means to kiss or have sex with someone. It is used by younger people.

Example: *I heard that Tilley and Adrian hooked up over the weekend!*

To get off with (someone) (UK): This usually means to (romantically) kiss someone.

Example: *Is it true that she got off with her best friend's boyfriend?*

To snog (UK): To (French) kiss someone. This could be seen as a slang term.

Example: *Her dad caught her snogging some boy in their sitting room.*

I was absolutely heart-broken but I knew then and there that I would break up with him. I thought about ringing on the doorbell and dumping him in person but I was so upset that I thought I couldn't handle it. So I pulled out my phone and took a picture of them kissing, and then emailed it to him with the message, 'you're dumped'. I never heard from him again and he stopped using the library so we never saw each other. It took a long time to get over it but I eventually got a boyfriend who apart from not sleeping around is also probably the love of my life. So it goes to show that there is a difference between real love and just plain old lust.

Vocabulary and Phrases:

To break up with someone: To end a relationship with someone. This can be either one person's action or a mutual decision.

Example 1: *I broke up with my girlfriend over the weekend.*

Example 2: *Me and my girlfriend decided to break up.*

To dump someone: To end a relationship with someone. This is when it is one person's decision. It has the feeling that the other person would be upset by it. It is not a polite phrase.

Example: *I don't know why but he always ends up dumping his girlfriends after a few months.*

The love of one's life: The main love in your entire life.

Example: *Even though I've had lots of relationships, I still think that my first boyfriend was the love of my life.*

To sleep around: To have lots of different sexual partners.

Example: *People who sleep around put themselves at more risk of catching STDs.*

Most TV dramas feature an element of romance but don't exclusively center around it. If you would like to just concentrate on this type of language then I suggest you watch films instead as there are a lot of 'Romance movies'. I also suggest that you watch 'Reality shows' such as 'Made in Chelsea' or if you can't find anything better 'Jersey shore' as 'relationships' are basically all they ever talk about.

HOSPITALS/MEDICINE

PART ONE

I've been working in a hospital for about a year. In this time I've pretty much gotten used to it, but at first I had no idea what was going on. I mean, everything was just so confusing. For instance, all of the job titles are strange. Of course I understood 'doctor' and 'nurse' but apart from that there are all these different levels and types. For example with the doctors there are obviously the surgeons and the other doctors but what is the difference? Also there are pediatricians, obgyns and midwifes. There are also cardiologists, oncologists and a ton of other types of doctor.

Vocabulary and Phrases:

Paediatricians : This is a doctor that deals with babies and children. This branch of medicine is called 'pediatrics'.

Example: *Tom's paediatrician says that he is getting better.*

OBGYN: This is a shortened term for obstetrics and gynecology. So it refers to a branch of medicine dealing with women/pregnancy.

Example: *The OBGYN told me that I needed to get as much rest as possible before the due date.*

A midwife: This is a person who deals with the actual birth of a child.

Example: *The midwife was very helpful and really helped the birth go as smoothly as possible.*

A cardiologist: This is a doctor that deals with heart problems. The branch of medicine is called 'cardiology'.

Example: *The cardiologist said that I would have to quit smoking and stop eating red meat if I wanted to reduce my chances of getting heart disease.*

An oncologist: This is a doctor that deals with cancer patients. The branch of medicine is called 'oncology'.

Example: *The oncologist had to break the news that the patient had cancer.*

Also, to make things even more confusing, within the doctors there are different levels of seniority. The new doctors are called residents, and are basically still doing their on-the-job-training. The next level up are the attendings who are the 'full' doctors and have totally finished their training.

Vocabulary and Phrases:

A resident: This is a newly graduated doctor who has to do on the job training. This training is called 'residency'.

Example: *The residents are the ones who have to work crazy hours but they don't tend to get paid that much.*

An attending: This is a doctor who has finished his on the job training.

Example: *The attendings have to teach the residents.*

Another thing that took me a long time to get used to was all of the jargon and specialised language. Here are a few of the words that they use regularly. A drip is called an 'I.V'. When they take someone's pulse and blood pressure they call that 'vitals'. When someone is having a heart attack they call that a 'cardiac arrest'. Another word they use is 'coding' which is when the heart has stopped. If someone 'flat lines', that means that their heart has stopped and that basically they are dead. Then they use the paddles and just before they electric shock the heart they shout "clear". Also, another word they often used was 'a central line' which is the tube they use to do *chemotherapy with.

*A cancer treatment.

Vocabulary and Phrases:

An IV/a drip: This is medicine that is delivered directly into the veins (**I**ntra**V**enously).

Example: *He couldn't eat or drink so they had to give him liquids via a drip.*

Vitals: This refers to 'vital signs' and are (according to Wikipedia) body temperature, pulse rate, blood pressure and respiratory rate.

Example: *The doctor checked the patient's vitals as soon as he got into the Emergency Room.*

Cardiac arrest: Heart attack.

Example: *He had a cardiac arrest so was rushed to hospital.*

Coding: This means that the patient's heart has stopped.

Example: *He's coding so we have to shock him.*

To flat line: This basically means when your heart stops beating. It refers to when the line on the heart monitor suddenly goes flat.

Example: *He flat lined during surgery but luckily the doctor was able to save him.*

'Clear!': In hospital dramas they always shout 'clear' when they are about to electric shock someone in order to get their heart stated again.

A central line: This is the tube they use to administer chemotherapy drugs.

Example: *The resident was learning how to set up a central line.*

Finally there were all of the different sections to the hospital. Firstly there are the wings, which are the main sections of the hospital building. Next are the wards which are sections of the hospital that deal with different medical problems. For example the 'oncology ward' and the 'pediatric ward'. Then there is the 'E.R' which is the emergency room, where they deal with all of the emergencies.

Vocabulary and Phrases:

A hospital wing: A large section of the hospital building.

Example: *Which wing is oncology in?*

A ward: This is a section in the hospital that deals with a certain branch of medicine.

Example: *Where is the oncology ward?*

The emergency room: This is the section where they deal with all of the emergencies.

Example: *The emergency room is a very stressful place to work.*

There are both hospital dramas and 'reality show hospital documentaries'

Hospital Dramas.

ER: This is a famous drama featuring George Clooney.

Grey's Anatomy: This show center's around a group of interns.

Scrubs: This is a comedy show that also centers around a group of interns.

Casualty: This is a UK show that is based in an emergency room.

Reality Documentaries.

24 hours on A&E: This show is based in an accident and emergency ward in a real UK hospital.

One Born Every Minute: This show is based in a maternity ward (where babies are born) in a real UK hospital.

SCHOOL

PART ONE

Most people look back at their school days with fondness, but not me. I absolutely hated school. I don't know exactly what it was but I just never really got into it. I think partly it was the fact that there were all of these cliques which I never really felt part of. Also there was real peer pressure to dress and act like everyone else. I used to dread going to school in the morning and I'd just spend the whole day waiting until the bell went so that I could finally go home.

Vocabulary and Phrases:

A clique: This is a small closed group of people. It is a negative term and describes a bit of a socially unhealthy group that doesn't like outsiders or doesn't treat non-group members well.

Example: *The problem with letting people choose which team to work on at work is that weird little cliques form.*

Peer pressure: This is when people of the same age or social background pressure you into doing something bad/you don't want to do. It is not always that they are forcing you, but more that everyone else is doing it so you feel that you should do it as well. For example if everyone else around you smokes then you might feel that you should start smoking as well.

Example: *I first started *shop lifting because of peer pressure. All of my friends were doing it so I just sort of naturally fell into it.*

*Stealing from shops.

The bell: This is the alarm that signals the beginning, breaks and end of the school day.

Example: *As soon as the end bell went I grabbed my bag and ran out of school.*

Part Two

I was pretty well behaved and was never suspended or excluded or anything like that, but I did used to bunk off a lot. I used to go to the local park and wait until it was time to go home and then pretend to my mother that I'd been at school all day. I remember that even though I loved the end of term because I didn't have to go to school over the holidays, I used to hate it because there was parent's evening, and my mum would discover my truancy. When I turned sixteen it was the happiest time in my life because I went to college* which was totally different from school.

*In the UK children finish school at 16 and then go to College for two years. This is the same as the US version, High School. Then at 18 they can go to University. This is what Americans often call 'College'.

Vocabulary and Phrases:

To be suspended: This is when a child has done something wrong and they are not allowed to come to school for a short period of time (a week or two). It is quite serious.

Example: *Tom was caught cheating on his homework so he was suspended for a week.*

To be excluded: This is when a child has done something really bad and is no longer allowed to attend that school. It is very serious.

Example: *Fiona was excluded for stealing school equipment.*

To bunk off (UK)/To play hooky (US): To not go to school even when you are supposed to.

Example 1: *I used to bunk off and go to the cinema instead.*

Example 2: *I used to play hooky and go to the movies instead.*

Parent's evening: This is when the parents of the students come in to discuss their child's progress with the teachers.

Example: *I've heard that most teachers absolutely hate parent's evening.*

Truancy: This is the more formal word for when a child 'bunks off'.

Example: *Truancy is a major problem in most UK schools.*

There are both school dramas and 'reality show hospital documentaries'.

Dramas.

Waterloo road:This is a UK drama based around the lives of students and teachers of a Scottish secondary school.

Teachers: This UK drama is based around the lives of a group of teachers at a secondary school.

Reality Documentaries.

Education Essex, Educating Yorkshire: Both of these shows are set in real schools and feature real students and teachers.

Sports

You should be familiar with a lot of the language connected to sports as it appears in most 'Elementary English' courses. However, there may be a few phrases that you are unfamiliar with so we will take a look at them now. We will also take a quick look at the specialized language for football/soccer as many of these words can be used for other sports as well.

Some words that you may not know:

Opponent: This is the person or team that you are competing against.

Example: *John's opponent in the Karate match was pretty good but John managed to win.*

Disqualification: This is when you are punished for doing something wrong and can no longer compete in the game or competition.

Example: *He was disqualified for punching below the belt.*

Steroids: These are a type of drug which enhance your physical performance. They are not allowed in sports competitions.

Example: *Everyone knew that he was taking steroids but nobody said anything.*

Endurance: This is when you keep going even if you are really tired. The ability to endure.

Example: *Marathon runners have amazing endurance.*

FOOTBALL/SOCCER

That was an absolutely amazing game. Jones played excellently and was able to get a hat-trick. Even though he got a yellow card in the first half he still went on to play a great game. The first goal was stunning, as he managed to dribble half way down the field, tackle past the keeper and then blast into the back of the net. The second goal was from a cross from the midfielder, it looked like he might be off side for a second but it was ok and he volleyed it right over the keeper's head. Towards the end of the match he was fouled and got a penalty, which he scored. It really was an exceptional performance from Jones this evening.

Vocabulary and Phrases:

A hat-trick: This is when one player scores three goals in one match.

Example: *The striker scored a hat-trick in the last 20 minutes of the game.*

A yellow/red card: This is a warning that the player gets from the referee if they do something wrong. If they get two yellow cards they will get sent off (they can't continue with the game). The red card is more serious. If they get that they will get sent off immediately.

Example 1: *Ok, that was his first yellow card. Let's hope that he doesn't get another one.*

Example 2: *It was such a dangerous tackle that he got a red card and was immediately sent off.*

To dribble the ball: This is when a player keeps kicking the ball over a distance and stays with the ball.

Example: *He dribbled the ball past the defender and then took a shot at goal.*

To tackle: This is when two opposing players try to get possession of the ball.

Example: *The other player managed to tackle the ball away from me.*

To cross the ball: This is when you pass the ball to another player on your team. It is often over quite a large distance.

Example: *He crossed the ball to me but the defender got to it first.*

The keeper: This means 'goal keeper', the player that defends the goal. They are also sometimes called the 'goalie'.

Example: *The keeper has had a great game and has made some excellent saves.*

To be off side (the off side rule): When the ball goes into play, the defense must be between the goal and the 'attacking' side. This rule is a little complicated but it stops players just waiting by the goal; they have to get past the other team's defense first.

Example: *The goal was not allowed because the striker was offside when the ball was passed to him.*

To volley (the ball): This is when the ball comes to you in the air and you kick it without it touching the ground.

Example: *He volleyed the ball right at the goal, but unfortunately the goalie (goal keeper) caught it.*

To foul: This is when one player physically obstructs/strikes another player.

Example: *He was a good player but he was always fouling, so he'd get sent off early.*

A penalty: If a player fouls or breaks the rules within their own goal keeper's box then the other team gets awarded a direct shot at goal. Also, if the game has no winner at the end, and there needs to be a winner, then they will have a penalty shootout to decide the winner.

Example: *If he scores this penalty they will win the game.*

Cars

Part One

Buying a car can be quite fun but it can also be a bit frustrating. Especially if you have no idea of what to look for. Last time I bought a car, instead of just looking for 'any' car, I decided to write out a check-list to help me get exactly what I was after.

Item One. Price: What type of car could I afford?

First I had to decide on the price range of the car I was looking for. I knew that if I spent too little I'd end up with a clapped out old banger which wouldn't be road worthy and definitely wouldn't pass its MOT. On the other hand if I bought a higher priced car I would have to take out financing which I definitely didn't want to do. So in the end I decided on a second hand car at the middle price range of the market.

Vocabulary and Phrases:

Price range: This is the space between the lowest and highest price you are willing to spend on an item.

Example: *I would like to buy a sports car but they're a little out of my price range.*

Clapped out (UK): This means old and probably close to the end of its usefulness.

Example 1: *My car is completely clapped out. It's time I brought a new one.*

Example 2: *I used to be good at sports, but I'm a bit clapped out now.*

An old banger: An old car which is in bad condition.

Example: *My dad always used to drive old bangers. Even if he had money to buy a decent car he never would.*

To be road worthy: When a car is in an acceptable condition to be driven on the road. It is not dangerous.

Example: *I kept on telling him that his car wasn't road worthy. It was no surprise when it broke down.*

M.O.T: This is a UK test to check that cars are safe to be on the road. All cars must 'pass their M.O.T' to get insurance, and you must have insurance to drive a car.

Example: *My car failed its M.O.T so it's going to cost a fortune to get it fixed.*

Financing: This is a loan to buy an expensive item. It is sometimes called 'HP' or 'hire purchase' in the UK.

Example: *I had to get financing to buy my car. I knew I couldn't afford it but I needed a decent car for work.*

A second hand car/a used car: This is a car which has been previously owned by someone else.

Example: *Buying a second hand car is always a risk as it may have problems that you don't know about.*

Item Two. What do you need the car for?:

There are lots of different makes and models of cars so it's important to choose one that suits your purposes. Do you want a coupe, a 4x4 or a hatchback? Maybe you want a nippy little run-around for just doing the shopping and going on short journeys. If you do I would suggest an automatic rather than a manual car. This is because if you are constantly speeding up and slowing down (like when you drive around town) it can be annoying constantly having to change gears. If on the other hand you are doing longer journeys, you may want a manual as they get more miles-per-gallon and you will save money on petrol. Also if you are going on long journeys you will want to be comfortable so it may be an idea to get a car with a high spec and lots of safety features such as airbags.

Vocabulary and Phrases:

Make and model: A 'make' is the 'brand' of car. The model is the 'version' of the car.

Example: *There are lots of makes and models of Japanese cars but I like the 'Hybrids'.*

A coupe: A two door car.

Example: *Coupes are not really suitable if you have children.*

A hatchback: A hatchback is a car which has a door at the very back that gives you access to the car. This is different to a trunk (US)/boot (UK), which is an enclosed storage compartment.

Example: *Hatchbacks are excellent for moving, because you can put the seats down for extra storage space.*

Nippy: Here this means small and quick. Very good at manoeuvring quickly.

Example: *I love small cars because they are so nippy.*

A run-around: A car that you use for short distances. A town car.

Example: *I just need a run-around for picking up the kids from school and doing the weekly shopping.*

An automatic car: A car that automatically changes gears for you.

Example: *I love automatic cars, all you have to do is point them in the right direction and then just press the pedal.*

A manual (UK)/ Stick (US): A car where you have to change the gears by yourself.

Example: *Manuals are much more popular in Europe than in America.*

To change gears: Cars have different 'driving modes' called 'gears'. For example if you are going slow or up a hill you want a low gear, but if you are going fast or on a flat road you will need a higher gear. So you need to 'change' between the 'gears'.

Example: *I like changing gears myself rather than using an automatic car. It gives me more of a feeling of control.*

Miles-per-gallon: This is how far the car can 'run' on a gallon of fuel. Sometimes called 'fuel consumption'.

Example: *How many miles-per-gallon can this car do?*

Petrol (UK)/ Gas (US): Fuel for cars etc.

Example: *They call petrol 'gas' in America.*

Spec (specifications): The details of the car. For example, the weight, size and safety features.

Example: *If you don't understand the car specs you should get a mechanic to explain them to you before you buy the car.*

An airbag: This is a safety feature. It is a bag that appears if you have a crash and stops you from hitting the front of your steering wheel and the window.

Example: *Having both driver's side and passenger airbags has saved a lot of lives.*

Item Three. Do you like it?

Once you have decided on the price range and roughly what type of car you want, you then need to take a few cars out for a spin to check their road handling. By that I mean, how fast do they accelerate? How well do they corner? Is it comfortable?

Once you have been through this check-list and taken a few cars out for a test drive you should be ready to make a decision.

Vocabulary and Phrases:

To take a car for a spin: This means to take a quick drive. Usually there is no real destination, you are just driving for fun.

Example: *I don't have anything to do this morning so why don't we take a quick spin around the countryside?*

Road handling: This is the performance of the car on the road.

Example 1: *The car scored top marks on road handling in that car magazine.*

Example 2: *This car handles pretty well in the rain.*

To accelerate: To increase speed.

Example: *This car accelerates really quickly.*

To corner: This is the verb used for turning corners.

Example: *This car corners pretty well.*

To test drive (a car): To take a car out for a drive before you decide to buy it.

Example: *You'd have to be crazy to buy a car without test driving it first. I mean, what if you didn't like it?*

If you are not particularly interested in cars then I would suggest that you watch Top Gear. This show is probably about the most popular car shows ever. Even people who hate cars like this show because it is so entertaining.

Youtube Car Channels.

Top Gear.

WILDLIFE

PART ONE

If someone says the word 'animal' I immediately think about a 'dog' or some other domesticated pet. After that I then think about different breeds of livestock roaming around on a rural farm somewhere. Then I might think of animals that I have seen in captivity such as lions and giraffes. I should imagine for a lot of people their experience of animals would be much the same as mine. So why are most television programmes about animals in the wild?

Vocabulary and Phrases:

Domesticated animals: These are animals that have been tamed by humans. This includes pets and animals that are used for food.

Example: *Probably the only non-domestic animal most people see on a daily basis are birds.*

A breed of animal: A type of animal. For example within cows there are lots of different 'types' or 'breeds'.

Example: *My favourite breed of dog is the dachshund.*

Livestock: These are animals that are bred for food. So, cows=beef, pigs=pork etc.

Example: *Most farms have one or two different breeds of livestock.*

Rural: This is an adjective meaning ‘countryside’.

Example: *I always wanted to live a rural lifestyle.*

In captivity: A ‘captive’ is ‘a prisoner’ or someone/thing that has been caught and is no longer free. So ‘captivity’ is when someone/thing is not free. Animals that are ‘in captivity’ are in zoos or wildlife parks and not in the wild.

Example: *I always feel bad when I see a huge animal like an elephant that is in captivity.*

I think it's because although most of us live relatively safe lives and actually like it that way, we all have a certain sense of adventure. So although we wouldn't like to meet a wild animal in real life, we do like seeing them on television. We love to watch programmes about <u>predators</u> <u>stalking</u> their <u>prey</u>, lions <u>roaring and growling</u> and eagles <u>soaring</u> in the air, because it excites a wonder in us. I think that although we do live safe lives, we also have <u>animal instincts.</u> So when we watch a programme about animals hunting in the wild we feel a weird mix of excitement and empathy for the prey. Even though we know that they will probably get caught and eaten we still hope that they will get away.

<u>Vocabulary and Phrases:</u>

A predator: An animal (or human) that hunts another.

Example: *Sharks are almost perfect predators.*

To stalk: To follow someone/thing (usually) secretly with the intention to attack them.

Example: *Wolves stalk their prey for hours before making the kill.*

Prey: This is the animal that is being hunted.

Example: *The prey often stands completely still hoping that the predator hasn't seen it.*

Roaring/growling: 'Roaring' is a loud noise that some animals make. Growling is a little quieter but still sounds aggressive.

Example: *I don't know what is more frightening, when the lion roared or growled.*

To soar: To increase in height very quickly. This is when a bird or a plane goes very high into the air very quickly.

Example: *Eagles soar into the air and then look for prey on the ground.*

Animal instincts: These are 'base' instincts that help animals stay safe from danger.

Example: *Even humans have some animal instincts that help us avoid danger.*

Nature

While there is a lot of terrible stuff on TV I think one of my favorite types of shows, are nature programmes. Of course there is nature all around us, especially if you live in the countryside but the programmes I particularly like are the ones that show beautiful, bountiful rain forests. Actually I watched a programme yesterday that was about a sanctuary for endangered species of plants. They are brought from all around the surrounding area in order to preserve them from ecological devastation and to save them from extinction.

Vocabulary and Phrases:

Bountiful: To have plenty of a good thing. It is often used in connection to plants that produce food.

Example: *It was a really bountiful harvest this year.*

A sanctuary: An area which is safe. These are areas that are made to protect certain things; animals, plants etc.

Example: *There is a very famous bird sanctuary near my house.*

Endangered species: Species (of animals and plants) that are in danger of dying out completely. Species that may become extinct if they are not protected.

Example: *There are thousands of endangered species in the Brazilian rainforest.*

To preserve (something): To save something. To maintain something so it remains in a good condition. A 'nature preserve' is an area specially for protecting nature or certain wild animals.

Example: *The purpose of a nature preserve is to help protect certain animals and plants.*

Ecological: This is a word to describe the natural environment.

Example: *The ecological effects of the oil spill have been devastating.*

Extinction: When a species or group completely dies out. No longer exists.

Example: *The Dodo is extinct.*

There are whole TV channels devoted to wildlife and nature programmes. For example National Geographic and the Discovery Channel.

Also I would recommend these BBC documentary series.

Planet Earth.

Nature/Wildlife Youtube Channels

Animal Planet.

National Wildlife.

Texas Parks and Wildlife.

BBC Earth.

MONEY

PART ONE

Are you one of those people who struggles to make ends meet? Are you facing large amounts of debt? This can be a frightening time. One of the most important things to remember is that you can overcome it. By using a proper budget you can cut down on your spending. The first thing you need to do is consider your income. Write down how much money you have coming in every month. Then note down what you need to buy and how much it all costs. Then you will see clearly how you can live within your means.

Vocabulary and Phrases:

To make ends meet: this is when you earn just enough money to live, but no more. You have no extra money left over after living expenses.

Example: Between my husband's and my wage we only just make ends meet.

To have debt/to be in debt: to owe money to someone/a bank etc. You need to re-pay someone money at one point.

Example 1: I have quite a lot of debt so there's no way I can quit my job at the moment.

Example 2: I'm in debt to the bank.

A budget/to budget: This is a fixed amount of money you have to spend on something. 'To budget' is when you are careful to only spend a certain amount of money.

Example 1: My budget for food shopping is about £50.

Example 2: I've had to budget a little this week as I had less money than I thought.

To cut down/back on (spending etc): to reduce how much you do something.

Example 1: I'm trying to cut back on how much I spend on alcohol.

Example 2: If you are putting on weight, try to cut down on how much bread you eat.

An income: money you earn from working, investments etc.

Example: My income is just about enough to live off of.

To have money coming in: this refers to the money you get every month from working/investments/people giving you money for other reasons etc. Basically all of the money you receive.

Example: Since my husband lost his job, the only money we have coming in is from my job.

To live within one's means: this is a phrase which means that you only use money that you have. You don't go into debt.

Example: I’ve always tried to live within my means, so I’ve never really had any debt.

You don't have to be tight fisted to be good with money. You just need to be prudent with your spending. For every purchase you make, consider whether you really need it. If you start cutting back on luxuries (going out drinking etc) you can afford more of the necessities (food etc) without having to borrow.

Vocabulary and Phrases:

To be tight fisted: this is when you do not like spending money. When you are mean with money. This is a negative term used about people who don't pay their share.

Example: I hate going out for dinner with my brother, he's so tight fisted. I always end up paying for everything.

To be good/bad with money: this is when you are good/bad at managing your own finances.

Example: She doesn't have a good job but because she is so good with money, she always seems to have more than enough.

To be prudent (with money): to be good with money. To be careful with money. To make good investments.

Example: He's been pretty prudent over the years and is now pretty well off.

Note: to be *'well off'* or *'wealthy'* means to have quite a lot of money.

To be able to afford (something): to have enough money to do/buy something.

Example 1: I've got a pretty good job so I can afford to eat out quite a lot.

Example 2: I can't afford to go out this weekend so I'll probably just stay at home and watch TV.

To borrow/lend: to borrow is when you take money from someone/a bank with the intention of giving it back. To lend is when you give money to someone but you want to get it back at a certain time.

Example 1: I had to borrow some money off of my parents in order to buy a car.

Example 2: I lent my son some money so he could buy a car.

Once you have become good at this process you can start to save money. To have some set aside allows you to prepare for when times might be tough. You can also have money saved for a rainy day. You might even save enough to have a nice nest egg for retirement. Having a good retirement fund can allow you to be generous to your children and grandchildren. Don't over-spend though. Even if you are loaded, if you spend more than you earn you will soon go broke.

Vocabulary and Phrases:

To have money set aside/tucked away: to have money saved.

Example 1: I have a bit of money set aside for emergencies.

Example 2: I have a bit of money tucked away to use for next year's summer holiday.

(Money that one is saving) for a rainy day: this is money you have saved 'just in case' you need it. Money for (future) difficult times.

Example: I have some money that I was saving for a rainy day. But I guess my situation is pretty bad now so I could use it.

A nest egg: this means 'savings of money'. Money you have saved for your future.

Example: I plan to use my nest egg as a deposit on buying a house.

To be generous: This is when someone is happy to give things to others. It refers to when people are happy to give money/time/energy etc.

Example: My mother is so generous, she is always offering to pay for everything.

To be loaded: to have lots of money. This is a very informal word.

Example: I heard that her new boyfriend is absolutely loaded.

Note: In American English 'loaded' can also mean 'drunk'.

To go broke/to be broke: this is when you have no money.

Example 1: My father went broke, trying to save his company.

Example 2: She was totally broke when she arrived in this country and now she is a millionaire.

We've all had times when we were only just scraping by. And there will always be moments when it is hard not to 'go through' money quickly. However, being frugal with your earnings can really help you save for those difficult times. You then won't need to borrow anything when times are tough. And if you are really frugal, you might even have a little extra.

Vocabulary and Phrases:

To be scraping by: to be just about surviving on the money you earn.

Example: Even though I love my job, I'm only just scraping by. So I'll probably have to get a new job pretty soon.

To 'go through' money: this is when you spend money easily.

Example: Even when I'm trying to be careful, I just go through money so easily. It just seems so expensive living in London.

To be frugal: This is when someone is very careful with money. It is not really a negative term but needs to be used carefully.

Example: He is so frugal that he uses teabags twice before throwing them away.

Earnings/to earn: money you make from working/ investments etc.

Example 1: She gives half of her earnings to charity.

Example 2: How much do you earn?

Extra Vocabulary:

To withdraw money: to take money out of the bank.

Example: Hi, I'd like to withdraw £100 please.

There are lots of programmes that talk about 'banking' and 'finance' but shows about everyday uses of money are not that common.

Money Youtube Channel:

Max Keiser: this is a very interesting and entertaining show about money and world finance.

JOB HUNTING

PART ONE

I have helped a lot of people find a job. The job market can be really tough sometimes and there is often stiff competition for the best jobs. Many people rely too much on their online job searches. Yet jobseekers should not just concentrate on this one method. One excellent way to find a job is to cold call companies. This is also known as a 'speculative application'. If you do look for work this way, you must be strong minded because you will often get turned down. However some employers think that people who go out contacting businesses and asking to be employed, actually show 'initiative' and they will sometimes employ these people.

Vocabulary and Phrases:

The job market: this refers to jobs that are on offer. Possible jobs that people can apply for.

Example: Since the recession started, the job market has been pretty slow.

Strong/stiff competition: this is when the other people applying for the same job as you, are quite good. You will have a hard time winning.

Example 1: I face pretty strong competition getting that job. All the other applicants have excellent qualifications.

Note: an 'applicant' is someone who applies for something.

Example 2: There's usually some pretty stiff competition for jobs like these.

An online job search: when you search for a job on the internet.

Example: Online job searches are more popular than looking in a newspaper. This is because they are constantly being updated online.

To cold call companies: to phone companies/people that you don't know. To try to sell something over the phone to people that you don't know.

Example: I absolutely hate cold calling people, as they usually don't want to speak to me.

To be turned down: to be rejected for something.

Example: I offered to help them improve their website but they turned me down.

When you do reach out to hiring companies there are a few rules you should follow. Even though lots of people do it, I'm actually against people who bend the truth on their applications. This may initially get them the job, but when they are actually working, they will find it tough. This could then lead to them being fired if the new employers find out that the person had lied on their application. Instead I have found that your CV / Resume should show your strong points without fabrication of facts (lying). You can shine in the job market by demonstrating your achievements in another position, rather than just providing a list of skills with no real evidence.

Vocabulary and Phrases:

To reach out to (someone/a company): to make contact with someone.

Example: I've reached out to a few companies but none of them are hiring at the moment.

To bend the truth: this is when you make something 'fit' into what is being asked of you. It is not exactly lying but it is not 100% truthful either. Many people do this when applying for jobs. For example if the job requires experience of training and you once helped train someone for a day at work. Then if you said that you had experience of 'training' then that is not a lie but it is not really what they meant. So you are not exactly lying but you are bending the truth.

Example: Everyone bends the truth when applying for a job.

C.V(Curriculum Vitae) (UK English)/Resume (US English): a document that lists your educational and work history.

Example: You should always make sure that your CV fits the job that you are applying for.

One's strong points: things about you that are attractive to an employer.

Example: His main strong point is that he has 10 years experience in sales.

To shine: to excel. To be obviously good at something. To be good at a particular thing.

Example: Since he moved into sales he has really started to shine.

A position: a job. A role.

Example: I had that position for 3 years, then I got promoted.

When writing a cover letter, I have often seen people just repeating what is in their CV. This is the wrong approach. Your cover letter should create a personable impression of you. At the same time you need to sell yourself by showing how you fulfill the criteria of the job specification. One thing that annoys me, and hiring managers alike, is the overuse of buzz words. If you use them correctly (but don't overuse them) you will impress the employer and may be asked in for an interview.

Vocabulary and Phrases:

A cover letter: a letter you write when you are applying for a job. This usually goes with your CV/resume or application. You use this to introduce and sell yourself.

Example: You should always include a cover letter when you apply for a job. This gives you an opportunity to really *sell* yourself.

To be personable: to be friendly/likable. To be easy to get on with.

Example: We are looking for someone quite personable to join our sales team.

To sell one's self: this is when you promote yourself. You make yourself or your services sound attractive so people will want to hire you or buy your services.

Example: To be honest he isn't very good at his job, but he's excellent at selling himself so he always gets hired.

To fulfill the criteria: to fit certain things expected in a job/role. For example, *you must have a degree, be under 35, and be willing to live abroad.*

Example: I fulfill the criteria for the job so there's a good chance that I'll get it.

Buzz words: these are special words or 'jargon' used for different fields.

Example: One of the most useful 'buzz words' when applying for a job is 'transferable skills'. This is when you adapt your current skills to a new task.

At the interview you need to have self-belief. That belief will give you positive body language and this will help you to stand out from the crowd. However, this will not guarantee that you excel in every interview you attend. I can think of countless applicants who have been the perfect fit and yet have failed to secure a position. This could just be because there was a better applicant, or there may be a less obvious reason. If this does happen to you, remember that the most important skill to have as a jobseeker is perseverance. Pick yourself up from disappointment and move on, that way you will succeed in finding a new job.

Vocabulary and Phrases:

To have self-belief: to have confidence in your own abilities.

Example: We try to help our employees develop self-belief.

Body language: this describes what your body's position and actions tell other people.

Example: When in an interview you should try to mirror the other person's body language.

To stand out: this is when you (or something) are better (or more special in some way) than the others.

Example: All of the applicants were good but the one that stood out for me was the lady who had done charity work in Africa.

To excel at something: to be very good at something.

Example: He really excels at sales, but isn't very good at managing other people.

A jobseeker (UK English): someone who is looking for a job.

Example: It's difficult being a jobseeker nowadays. All the jobs ask for so many qualifications.

Perseverance/to persevere: to keep going. To not quit.

Example 1: Perseverance is one of the main things we look for in our employees.

Example 2: You need to persevere if you want to succeed in business.

EXTRA PRACTICE.

There are lots of different shows about work but the best one about actually getting a job is The Apprentice. It's a competition where lots of different people are competing for the same job.

Job Hunting Youtube Channel:

Tampa Bay Community Network: This channel has a lot of videos on job hunting.

FILMS

PART ONE

If there is one thing that I really love to do, it's watching films. Sometimes I just want to kill a bit of time and watch anything, but other times I'll search around to find a specific film that interests me. I don't really prefer any one genre (though I do like chick-flicks!). Any film can be included within my film collection or on my favourites list. I can find value and entertainment even in films that are not directed towards me. For example, even though action films are sometimes thought to be dumbed-down, some of them can be very thought provoking. The most important thing for me is not the 'type' of film it is, but whether there is a good story and if it has good performances from the actors.

Vocabulary and Phrases:

To kill time: this is when you have some spare time and you do a non-important activity to fill it.

Example: We had some time to kill so we went to the marina to look at all of the boats.

A genre: a type of film/book. For example 'action' 'romance' 'comedy' are all film genres.

Example: My favourite genre of film is probably thrillers.

A chick flick: a film that is aimed at a female audience.

Example: *Thelma and Louise* was the first chick flick that I ever saw.

To dumb (something) down: to make something easy to understand. This is a negative term and refers to the media 'making people stupid' by never having difficult themes.

Example: I've stopped watching the news on TV. It's just so dumbed down. I'd rather read a newspaper.

To be thought provoking: something that causes you think about a certain topic.

Example: That documentary was really thought provoking. I couldn't stop thinking about it for days afterwards.

A good/bad performance: an actor's 'performance' is how they played the character.

Example: That actor's performances are always pretty good, even if the films are not that good.

Often the actor's performance relies on who is at the helm of the movie. That is probably why many of the films I enjoy are all done by the same directors and producers. The right director can ensure that the audience will be engrossed in their film. The wrong person in charge can turn a promising plot into a flop.

Vocabulary and Phrases:

To be 'at the helm': this describes the director's role in the film. For example, if you say that 'Jenny Smith is at the helm of the new monster movie' then you mean that 'Jenny Smith is the director of the new monster movie'.

Example: After the success of the first movie, everyone hopes that the same director will be at the helm for the sequel.

Note: 'a sequel' is the second, third etc film in a series.

To be engrossed in (something): to enjoy/be interested in something so much that you forget about/don't think about other things.

Example: He was so engrossed in his book that he forgot to get off of the train and missed his stop.

A plot: the story of a film, book or TV show.

Example: I hated that film. It was just action, there was absolutely no plot!

A flop: a film that performs financially badly .

Example: That film was supposed to be a blockbuster but it completely flopped.

Yet even with the wrong leadership there can be those actors who will always steal the show. These actors will often leave the 'turkey' of their career behind and move on to better things. It is great to see these actors develop their careers over time and that is why I love to watch straight to DVD films. Often the stars of the future can be found hiding in these lower budget independent movies.

Vocabulary and Phrases:

To steal the show: when an actor/actress 'steals the show', it means that they had the best performance. They were the best thing about the film.

Example: All the actors were great but I think that the kid really stole the show.

A turkey: a film that was critically unsuccessful.

Example: That film was a complete turkey. It was panned by the critics.

Note: to be *panned by critics* means that film critics (in newspapers etc) absolutely hated the film.

Straight to DVD: this refers to a film that did not have a theatrical release but instead was only released on DVD.

Note: a 'theatrical release' is when a film is released at the cinema.

Example: That film was 'straight to DVD' so it may not be very good.

A low budget film/a big budget film: a film that was cheap/expensive to make.

Example: some of the best films I've ever seen have actually been pretty low budget.

An independent (film): a film not produced by a major studio.

Example: I prefer independent films as the writing is usually a lot better.

I find it interesting how a movie which has a good premier and good reviews can sometimes bomb at the box office. You can often tell which films these are going to be by how much they make on the opening weekend. If they don't make much then, they will rarely succeed.

Vocabulary and Phrases:

A premier: the first time a film is shown at the cinema.

Example: I went to the film's premier and got to meet all of the stars of the movie.

To bomb at the box office: the 'box office' refers to how much money a film made. So when a film 'bombs at the box office', it did very badly financially.

Example: Even though the critics really liked that film, it totally bombed at the box office.

Opening weekend: this refers to the first weekend a new film shows at the cinema. It is often mentioned when discussing how well a film has done financially.

Example: That film did pretty well on its opening weekend.

However, not every film which fails at the cinema is a bad film in my opinion. One classic is Sleeping Beauty, which actually did very poorly for Disney. Yet for many children this can be great escapism and addictive viewing on a Sunday afternoon. Therefore no matter how successful it is, or whether it is a romcom or an action movie; I will give every movie a chance.

Vocabulary and Phrases:

Escapism: this describes when someone uses entertainment to escape reality. It is not a negative term. It just describes going into one's imagination rather than reality.

Example: I love that show because it's pure escapism. I hate shows that are just like real life.

To be addictive: to make you want to watch more and more.

Example: That show is so addictive, I can't stop watching it.

A romcom: a romantic comedy.

Example: That actress is always in romcoms.

More Vocabulary and Phrases:

A blockbuster: a very popular film that makes a lot of money.

Example: Most blockbusters seem to be re-makes of old films nowadays.

Youtube Film Review Channels:

Breakin it Down

What the Flick?!

Epic Movie Review

Alcohol

Part One

There are many people out there who enjoy alcohol. I am not one of those people, I am tea total. Don't get me wrong, although I don't understand heavy drinkers, I am not judging others who enjoy a drink now and then, or even the occasional nightcap. I even kind of respect the knowledge involved in becoming a wine connoisseur. I have just simply decided to be on the wagon and not join in. I would rather be sober than drink alcohol, if only because I don't have to deal with hangovers.

Vocabulary and Phrases:

To be a tea totaller/to be tea total: to not drink alcohol.

Example1: He's a tea totaller so he probably won't want this bottle of wine.

Example 2: I've been tea total ever since university. I just don't like drinking that much.

To be a heavy drinker: to drink a lot of alcohol. To drink often and a lot.

Example: I wouldn't say that he was an alcoholic but he is a heavy drinker.

A nightcap: a quick drink before going to bed. A quick drink at the end of the night.

Example: Do you fancy a nightcap before you leave?

A (wine) connoisseur: someone who knows a lot about wine/alcohol.

Example: I'm not a connoisseur but I know what I like.

To be on the wagon: to have stopped drinking. To not be drinking alcohol for a period of time.

Example: I'm on the wagon so I won't be joining you at the pub.

To be sober: to not be drunk. To have not drunken alcohol.

Example: I'm totally sober so I'll do the driving.

To have a hangover/to be hung over: to feel tired and sick the next day after drinking.

Example 1: I've got a hangover after last night's party.

Example 2: I'm totally hung over after last night's party.

A recent trend amongst young people is 'binge drinking'. This is when you drink lots and lots in a very short period of time. Young women in particular are doing this more and more. One of my daughter's friends could literally drink anyone under the table. Of course I know that they are young and probably enjoy drinking games and having fun with their friends, but I worry that binge drinking is a small step towards being an alcoholic.

Vocabulary and Phrases:

Binge drinking/a binge drinker: someone who drinks a lot in a short period of time. For example if you don't drink during the week but then drink loads and loads over the weekend then this is 'binge drinking'.

Example: Binge drinking is becoming very common amongst young women in Britain.

To drink someone under the table: this is when you have a stronger resistance to alcohol than someone else. You are less affected by alcohol than someone else.

Example: Even though I am small, I can still drink most of my friends under the table.

Note: someone who has a weak resistance to alcohol is sometimes called 'a lightweight'. This is not a very polite term.

Drinking games: these are games where the loser has to drink alcohol.

Example: I enjoy drinking games because the more you lose the more fun it is!

To be an alcoholic: to have physical/mental addiction to alcohol.

Example: He's a recovering alcoholic so it's best not to offer him anything to drink.

I also find very heavy drinkers quite hard to deal with. I think this started with an ex-boyfriend of mine. He started off as a social drinker, getting tipsy now and again. But then due to stress he started drinking a lot and going on benders every week. He'd come home completely out of it after being out drinking. I asked him to stop and he did for a bit. But then after a while he'd be down the pub again downing drinks and coming home totally pissed. I left him after a few months of this and ever since have tried to avoid people who drink all the time.

Vocabulary and Phrases:

A social drinker: someone who only drinks on social occasions.

Example: I'm basically just a social drinker. I only drink when I'm out with friends.

To be tipsy: to be a little bit drunk.

Example: I was a bit tipsy but not drunk.

To go on a bender (UK English): this is slang which means 'to drink a lot over a period of a few days-weeks. **Be very careful** with this word as it has other very offensive meanings.

Example: I went on a bit of a bender over the weekend and now feel absolutely terrible.

To be out of it: this is when you are so drunk that you don't know what is going on.

Example: That guy was so out of it, he couldn't even stand up properly.

To down a drink: this is when you drink a glass of alcohol in one go. You drink something without stopping.

Example: I got a call from a friend so I just downed my drink and then went off to meet him.

To be pissed (UK English): to be very drunk. This is not a polite term.

Example: He was completely pissed at his birthday party. It was pretty funny.

However, not drinking doesn't mean I am left out at a party. When there is a toast to be made, I simply have a soft drink instead. This doesn't spoil my fun at all, it just means that I can remember the fun times and will have no regrets in the morning.

Vocabulary and Phrases:

To make a toast: to give a speech about something while drinking.

Example: During weddings, it's usual for the best man to make a toast of some kind.

PARENTING

PART ONE

Being a parent is a wonderful experience. I have been a parent more than once and I can honestly say that each experience is different. With your first child it is quite normal to be over-protective. You often want to do what the parenting books tell you. Yet I have found that wrapping your child up in cotton wool will spoil your fun and theirs. When it comes to your second child you tend to be more laid back than with your first. Though in my opinion you should always have a hands on approach with parenting.

Vocabulary and Phrases:

To be over-protective: to try and protect your child from everything even if they need to learn from difficult situations.

Example: I try not to be over-protective of my kids because I want them to be strong adults in the future.

To wrap someone up in cotton wool: this is when you protect someone (usually your child) from the world. This is a negative term and means that you are making the child weak and unable to cope with the real world.

Example: Her parents completely wrapped her up in cotton wool when she was younger. So now she has absolutely no life skills.

To be laid back: to have a relaxed attitude about things.

Example: My dad was pretty laid back about everything except bedtimes. We had to be in bed by 7pm exactly.

To have a hands on/off approach (to parenting): this describes being involved/not involved with bringing up children. To be hands on, means that you take an active role. To be hands off you are not so involved.

Example 1: My mum had a hands off approach to parenting. She basically let us do whatever we liked as long as we didn't hurt ourselves.

Example 2: She has a very hands on approach. She is very interested in her children's lives.

PART TWO

The best tool any father/mother will have is their paternal/maternal instinct. This has always told me the right thing to do. I've always believed that a paternal/maternal instinct exists whether you are part of a nuclear family, or a step-parent ,foster parent or adoptive parent. This must be true because there are plenty of excellent step/foster/adoptive parents out there.

Vocabulary and Phrases:

Paternal/maternal: 'paternal' refers to the father role and 'maternal' refers to the mother role.

Example 1: I do want kids at one point but I'm not really the maternal type.

Example 2: Most mothers have natural maternal instincts.

Example 3: There was never a real paternal figure in my life.

A nuclear family: this is a 'typical' family of 'mother, father and two kids'.

Example: The 'nuclear family is becoming less and less common nowadays.

A step parent: when your mother/father remarries someone else, then that person is your step parent.

Example: I actually really liked my step-mum.

A foster parent: someone who looks after a child temporarily. A foster parent is not an adoptive parent. It is more like someone who looks after a child full-time like a parent but it is a paid job.

Example: I still see my foster parents now, even though I stopped living with them when I was 12.

Adoptive parents: to adopt a child is to take legal and permanent responsibility of a child. They are not the 'birth parents' but they are the 'legal' parents of the child.

Example: I didn't know that my parents were actually my adoptive parents until I was about 8 years old.

One of the biggest challenges any parent will have is when they have to discipline their children. Sometimes you can feel cruel telling off one of your off-spring. Yet this is an important part of being a parent. There are many different punishments you can give for bad behaviour, including imposing a curfew or grounding your child. These sound great in theory, but I've always questioned their effectiveness. Does it really make your child *understand* what they have done wrong? Also these punishments only work for older children, for example you can't ground a toddler!

Vocabulary and Phrases:

To discipline (a child): to punish a child for being naughty. This is not a common phrase.

Example: My father was pretty strict, he'd discipline us if we were naughty.

To tell (someone) off: to tell someone that they have done something bad.

Example: I hated school, I was always being told off by the teacher.

Off-spring: your children.

Example: I don't have any off-spring.

A curfew: a certain time that a child has to be back in the house by.

Example: I never really had a curfew but I didn’t go out much in the evenings anyway.

To ground (a child): when a child has been very naughty the parents sometimes ‘ground’ them. This is when (except for school) they are not allowed to go out of the house.

Example: I can’t go to the party this weekend because I’m grounded.

A toddler: a child between 2-4 years old.

Example: toddlers are definitely the hardest to look after.

Whatever way you punish a child you must ensure that you are consistent. To give one sibling one punishment and a different punishment to another will only create problems. I have also found that praise can be a more effective method of encouraging good behaviour. If a child is told when something is good and rewarded, they are more likely to carry on with that behaviour. Though I have often found that parents sometimes forget about this parenting style and go straight to the punishments.

Vocabulary and Phrases:

Sibling: brother/sister.

Example: I don't have any siblings. I'm an only child.

To praise someone: to tell someone that they have done something well.

Example: If you praise your child often they will gain confidence.

Being a parent is a fantastic responsibility and if you bring your child up to have the right attitude in life you have done well. Then as they become adults themselves you will have given them the best inheritance in life: a good upbringing.

Vocabulary and Phrases:

To bring someone up to (do something): This is when you raise a child to act in a certain way.

Example: I have brought my kids up to be polite.

An inheritance/to inherit: when you get money/property etc from your parents after they die. **Note:** in the article above the word 'inherit' is used in connection with 'attitude' this is fine as well.

Example 1: I inherited the house after my parents died.

Example 2: My parents were pretty poor so I didn't get an inheritance.

Youtube Parenting Channels:

Parent's Magazine

Isis Parenting

Social Media

Part One

Social media has been around for a long time now. When people first started using social media they thought it would be a fad. However, it is safe to say it is more popular now than ever. There are lots of these different networking sites and they all have different uses. Some social media platforms can be used to help search for a job whereas others are best for keeping in contact with friends and family.

Vocabulary and Phrases:

A fad: something that is only popular for a short period of time.

Example: Everyone thought that dance music was a fad but it is now more popular than ever.

To network: this is when you meet lots of different people on purpose in order to get clients and make good business (etc) connections.

Example: I try to spend a few hours a week networking. This not only helps me find new clients, but new suppliers as well.

To keep in contact (with someone): To maintain a relationship with someone.

Example: I use social media to keep in contact with people.

For me, Twitter* is like a news site. People post short messages to each other in order to involve them in a larger conversation. Many of the messages will lead you to a long blog post which can sometimes be quite interesting. Businesses do this a lot to attract customers to their website and give them details about their latest products. Others will use the micro-blogging site to have conversations in short form. Twitter is very good for keeping up with the latest trending topics as it is quick to respond to changes.

*Twitter is a site where you can leave very short messages and people can follow you and reply to you.

Vocabulary and Phrases:

To post messages/something on the internet: this is when you write something (or comment on something) on the internet.

Example 1: I posted a message on his Facebook page.

Example 2: I posted a comment on her blog.

To attract customers: To do something that will make customers come to you.

Example: There are lots of good ways to attract customers but one of the best is to offer a discount.

Micro-blogging sites: these are like blogs but the messages are shorter.

Example: Twitter is a very popular micro-blogging site.

To keep up (with something)/to keep up to date with something: this is when you closely follow what is happening in a certain field. You know what developments are taking place.

Example 1: I try to keep up with what is happening in the fashion world.

Example 2: The best way to keep up to date with what is happening in the world is to get your news from the internet.

To be trending (on twitter): a topic that is being talked about a lot on twitter.

Example: I hear that that singer is trending on twitter right now.

The most effective site to stay connected is probably Facebook. Status updates and 'liking' someone's page are the best ways to ensure that you are kept up-to-date with your friends and family. Facebook is the largest network and has been around for a long time. It is often a misconception that it always gives up-to-the minute information. Sometimes the updates on a newsfeed are days or weeks old. This can be confusing for the reader.

Vocabulary and Phrases:

To stay connected : to stay in touch/in contact with someone.

Example: I find that the best way to stay connected nowadays is to join a social networking site.

Status updates: new information about you that you post on your Facebook page.

Example: I always forget to update my status on Facebook so it still says that I am married, even though I got divorced 3 years ago.

To like someone's page: this is when you tick a box on someone's Facebook page that says that you like something they have posted.

Up-to-the minute: very up to date.

Example: I want up to the minute reports on what is happening.

LinkedIn is sometimes considered the professional's social media network. This is because the network is often used by jobseekers and businesses for the job market. Though any site can be used to recruit people, LinkedIn is the natural choice. The personal profiles are like CVs and resumes, and people can recommend you based on your skills. This makes LinkedIn a powerful, yet sometimes underused social media network.

Vocabulary and Phrases:

A personal profile: this is a short written description of yourself.

Example: It's best to have a personal profile if you want to use social media to promote yourself.

(When someone) recommends you: this is when someone says that you would be suitable for a certain job etc.

Example: Someone recommended me on LinkedIn and now I have a new client.

FRIENDSHIP

PART ONE

Unfortunately, I've always had trouble making friends. I don't know what it is about me. I would meet someone and really feel that we were getting on and that we could be friends. But then we would just naturally start to drift apart and I'd never see them again. Or I'd try to make friends or join a 'clique' but it would always end the same way. They'd find out that I had nothing in common with them and that would be the end of that. This happened to me time and again throughout my childhood. This all stopped when I went to university and met Susannah. From the moment we met we immediately hit it off and we have been friends ever since.

Vocabulary and Phrases:

To get on with someone: to have a good relationship with someone.

Example: I get on with most of the people in my family.

To drift apart: to slowly stop having a relationship with someone. This is not because of an argument, it is just that you naturally stopped seeing this person. Or that you naturally just stopped having things in common with this person.

Example: After I left university I sort of just drifted apart from most of my friends there.

A clique: a small group of people. This is a negative term and describes a group which doesn't really like/accept outsiders.

Example: I hated school. There were too many cliques, and I always felt lonely.

To have things in common (with someone): to have similar interests. To have similar tastes. To have a similar background.

Example: I stopped going to that club because I found that I don't have that much in common with the other people.

To hit it off with someone: this is when you meet a new person and immediately have a friendly relationship with them. To immediately like each other.

Example: I met her at a training session. Because we hit it off immediately we decided to stay in touch.

Nowadays me and Sussanah speak on the phone almost every day. We've been through through thick and thin together and share everything. Anyway, a few days ago she told me about some issues she'd been having with her friends. Even though we are good friends we kind of have separate social groups. Anyway, it seems that she had fallen out with a few people. I asked her why, and she said it was mainly because she felt that she was the only one making an effort to keep in touch. She'd tried to make up with them afterwards but there was still some bad feelings between them.

Vocabulary and Phrases:

Through thick and thin: this phrase means that you have gone though both good and bad situations with this person. You have survived all situations with this person/company.

Example: My wife has stuck with me through thick and thin. Even when I lost my job and we went into debt, she was always positive and supported me.

A social group: a group of your friends. This is a group that all know each other, not lots of individual friends.

Example: I have quite a mixed social group. There are men and women, professionals and students.

To fall out with (someone): when you have a disagreement with someone. When after a disagreement you either temporarily or permanently don't have a relationship with someone.

Example 1: I fell out with my brother when we were about 20, but we are friends again now.

Example 2: Me and my business partner fell out over money. Unfortunately this meant that we could no longer work together.

To keep in touch/to lose touch (with someone): to keep in contact with someone/to stop keeping in contact with someone.

Example 1: I keep in touch with my old friends via email.

Example 2: Over the years I've lost touch with most of my school friends, but I still see James pretty regularly.

To make up with (someone): this is when you have had a disagreement with someone but have now become friends again.

Example: Even though I often argue with my husband we always make up afterwards.

I <u>empathized</u> with her because the same thing happened to me a few years before. One of my <u>buddies</u> from work and I were <u>inseparable</u> for the longest time. Still, our <u>relationship</u> slowly fell apart. I thought he would be my <u>lifelong friend</u>, but we kind of lost touch after I got a new job.

<u>Vocabulary and Phrases:</u>

To have empathy/to empathize (with someone): to understand how other people feel about something.

Example: If you want to work for this charity you must have a lot of empathy for the people we deal with.

A Buddy: this can either mean 'a mate' or 'a friend'.

Example: He's one of my university buddies.

To be inseparable: to always be with a certain person.

Example: Me and my best friend were inseparable until my family had to move to another town.

A relationship: a connection between people. Social interaction over a period of time.

Example: I have problems trusting people, so relationships are difficult.

A lifelong friend: A person you have been friends with your whole life.

Example: I started a business with my lifelong friend.

"Maybe this is a good thing, Susannah," I said. "If no one else is making the effort, then you should just give them some space and see how it goes. Just keep them as acquaintances for now. They'll either try to make amends or they won't. There's nothing you can really do now". The advice was harsh, but she understood. Sometimes you just have to let people go.

Vocabulary and Phrases:

To give people/someone space: to give someone time to think about something. To not put pressure on someone. To not see someone, so they can calm down/forgive you etc.

Example: If you have a big fight with someone it's best to give them a little space so they can calm down.

An acquaintance: a person that you know but you are not friends with. This is not a negative term. You *may* or *may not* like this person.

Example: I don't really know him. He's just an acquaintance from work.

To make amends: to make up with someone. To repair a broken relationship.

Example: We had be fighting for so long that I'd forgotten what the cause of it all was. I felt that it was time that we made amends.

Extra Vocabulary and Phrases:

A pal: this can either mean 'a mate' or 'a friend'.

Example: She's been a pretty good pal over the years.

A companion: this describes a person (or pet) that is company for you. It is a more descriptive way to say 'friend'. This is a difficult word to use correctly.

Example: She's been a good companion over the years.

To be social: to enjoy mixing with people/friends.

Example: My husband is a lot more social than me. He likes to go out while I prefer to stay at home.

To hang out with (someone): to spend time with someone. This phrase is often used by younger people.

Example: Since I got my new job, I've had no time to hang out with my friends.

To touch base (with someone): to meet/speak with a friend (business acquaintance) and share news.

Example: It was good to touch base with Tim last night. It seems that he's been pretty busy recently.

Mates: this word is usually used in the UK and means 'someone who you are friendly with'. Not exactly a friend, but definitely someone who you enjoy spending time with.

Example: He's a pretty good mate. I wouldn't keep in contact with him if I moved town, but it's nice to go to the pub with him occasionally.

Extra Practice.

There are many different shows that feature friends but I would suggest the comedy ‘Friends’, as it is both funny and the language is a perfect level for intermediate English learners. Also you might try ‘Made in Chelsea’ as it is a reality show that centres around a group of friends.

FAMILY

PART ONE

A few years back when I was working in a local shop, I saw a girl who looked exactly like me. We both looked at each other for a minute in confusion. "Wow," I said. "This is a little weird." After talking for a few minutes, we decided to meet after I got out of work. It turned out that she was my long lost twin sister! My parents had put her up for adoption when we were born. I didn't have any other siblings, so it was exciting meeting Lucy.

Vocabulary and Phrases:

One's long lost (brother/sister etc): a family member that you lost contact with and have now found again.

Example: Because of facebook I was able to find my long lost brother.

To put a child up for adoption: this is when you can no longer look after a child and let someone adopt the child.

Example: I was put up for adoption when I was very young so I can't remember my birth mother.

Siblings: brothers and sisters.

Example: I was an only child but I always really wanted to have siblings.

Part Two

Lucy and I talked all the time. One night when I stayed over at her house, she told me all about how dysfunctional her family was. She was adopted by a huge family that was spread all over the country. The oddest thing about them was that they all shared the same blonde hair. "It's a family trait," Lucy explained. "My red hair is really obvious at family reunions, so I stay with people who aren't blood relatives, like my cousin's wife. *Not that I go to the reunions anymore.*"

Vocabulary and Phrases:

A dysfunctional family: a family that that has serious problems.

Example: Even though she comes from a dysfunctional family, she has become an excellent mother.

A family trait: this is when members of the same family have the same personality or physical points.
Example: Both me and my mother get angry very quickly. It's a bit of a family trait.

A family reunion: When members of your family get together. This is usually for special occasions.

Example: Everyone in my family lives in different countries but we try to have a family reunion every few years.

Blood relatives: people who are directly related to you. Not family members through marriage etc.
Example: She's not a blood relative but I really feel close to my step mum.

"What happened?" I asked. I come from a very tight-knit family and couldn't imagine not going to a reunion. It was the only time I got to see some of my distant relatives.

She said "You know that phrase 'blood is thicker than water'?" I nodded. "They believe that. A man I was dating proposed to me two or three years ago, only a few months after my uncle died. I said yes, and I wanted to go around the world with my new spouse... With my uncle gone, my dad was depressed and wanted me to stay instead. He was estranged from his wife, (my mum), and would be left all alone. 'You can't leave your father like this,' my widowed aunt said. 'He needs you now.' I guess it was selfish of me to go, but I did it anyway. My mum had left him as well. Like mother like daughter, I guess".

Vocabulary and Phrases:

A close/tight knit family: a family that has a close relationship.

Example: My family used to be pretty close knit, but after my parents died, we all slowly stopped seeing each other.

Distant relatives: these are family members that are not closely connected to you (for example, your grandfather's brother's children).

Example: It's a bit of a coincidence, but my new boss is actually a distant relative of mine.

Blood is thicker than water: this is a phrase which means that the connection between family members is stronger than that between friends etc. It is now often used to mean that 'the connection between family members is strong'.

Example 1: If I had to choose between my friend and my brother, I would choose my brother. In the end, blood is thicker than water.

Example 2: In the end 'blood is thicker than water' so I had to forgive my brother.

A spouse: a husband or wife.

Example: What's the name of his spouse again?

An estranged (brother/sister etc): this describes a person you used to have a relationship with but are no longer friendly with. You actively *don't like* this person.

Example 1: Me and my brother have been estranged for some time now.

Example 2: She is trying to repair her relationship with her estranged son.

A widow/widower: someone whose husband/wife has died.

Example 1: She's a widow, her husband died last year.

Example 2: He's a widower, his wife died last year.

Like father/mother like son/daughter: this is when both father and son (mother and daughter) have similar personalities/characteristics.

Example: It seems that that her daughter is also good at maths. Like mother like daughter.

"I became the black sheep of the family after that. The funny thing was that it wasn't even worth it. He divorced me only a few months later because my in-laws didn't like me. After that my mum and I moved here to try to start a new life and forget about our ex-husbands. As nice as it is being independent, I do miss some of my extended family. I guess meeting you makes up for that!"

Vocabulary and Phrases:

The black sheep of the family: the person (usually one of the adult children) in a family that doesn't really fit in. They go away and do their own thing.

Example: All my brothers joined the family firm, but I was always the black sheep so I moved to South America and started my own company.

In-laws: these are your husband's or wife's parents,

Example 1: I really like my mother in law.

Example 2: I am going to meet my in-laws for the first time this weekend.

An ex-husband/wife: a husband/wife that you are divorced from.

Example: I still keep in contact with my ex-wife.

An extended family: your 'immediate family' are your parents and siblings and grandparents. Your extended family are members who you are not connected as closely to. For example, cousins etc.

Example: I have a massive extended family, so it is really expensive over Christmas.

Extra Vocabulary and Phrases:

Relatives: family members.

Example: I usually have all of my relatives over for supper once a year.

A partner: this is sometimes used to mean a romantic partner (not married). A long-term boyfriend/girlfriend.

Example: They are not married, but my sister and her partner have been living together for about 10 years.

Extra Practice

There are lots of shows that feature families but the one you should start with is 'Brothers and Sisters' as it is 100% about a family and they will use a lot of the language featured in this chapter.

PERSONALITY

PART ONE

As a senior at River High School, I'm allowed to drive myself to school, but that means I come to school late a lot. The traffic is really bad if you leave at the wrong time. Thankfully, my teacher is really <u>easy going</u>. She never gives me trouble for coming in late. It's probably because I'm such a <u>diligent</u> student. I always do my homework and class work. There are a lot of students who get better grades than me on tests and are really smart, like Allison, but even though she's clever she's not a very nice person. I once over-heard the teachers saying that she was '<u>a piece of work</u>' and that she was perhaps the most <u>self centred</u> student they had ever met!

<u>Vocabulary and Phrases:</u>

To be easy going: to have a relaxed attitude. To not be strict in your lifestyle.

Example: My mother was pretty easy going, but my father was very strict.

To be diligent: to be hard working.

Example: I wasn't a very diligent student. I used to bunk off all of the time.

To be a piece of work: this describes a very unpleasant person.

Example: My boss is a real piece of work. She is always shouting at everyone.

To be self centred: to be selfish. To only think about yourself.

Example: Even though he has kids he spends all of his money on nice clothes for himself, while his kids look pretty dirty. He's so self centred.

My art class is pretty terrible to tell you the truth. The first time I met the art teacher we got off on the wrong foot. She's completely hardnosed and even if she says something nice about my work she always has this really passive aggressive way of saying it. She's a nutcase like most artists, but she can also be rude at times. I'm a more outgoing person who enjoys talking with other students. You'd think that you could talk all you want in an art class, right? Wrong! We have to sit in absolute silence in her class. It's as if she thinks that if you are extroverted you will not be any good at art.

Vocabulary and Phrases:

To get off on the wrong foot: to have an unfriendly start to a relationship. When the first time you meet someone doesn't go well.

Note: this is not really a 'personality' phrase, but it is useful.

Example: Even though we got off on the wrong foot, we are friends now.

To be hardnosed: to be unfeeling. To not care too much about the affect of your actions on other people.

Example: My boss is so hardnosed. He doesn't care if people lose their jobs as long as he can make a profit.

Passive aggressive: this describes someone who pretends to be nice but is actually quite aggressive. So they say something that seems ok but the real meaning is a bit nasty.

Example 1: She's such a passive aggressive. You never really know what she's thinking.

Example 2: Even when it seems that he is being nice, if you listen to what he is actually saying, the meaning is quite rude.

A nutcase: a crazy person. This is not polite.

Example: I liked him at first, but to be honest he's a bit of a nutcase so I avoid him now.

To be outgoing: to enjoy speaking to people. To enjoy going out and doing things.

Example: I'm pretty outgoing. Whenever I move house I make friends pretty quickly.

To be extroverted: to have an outward personality. To like speaking to people and being in social situations.

Example 1: He's such an extrovert, he even speaks to people he doesn't know on the street.

Example 2: My wife is very extroverted, she loves wearing crazy colours and going to parties.

In that class, Steve sits next to me. He's always been really introverted, shy, and modest, but he's an amazing painter. The teacher is always criticizing every choice he makes and can be so domineering. Just a few days ago, he shocked the whole class by *standing up to** the teacher for once. We started talking to him more after that, and I was happy to see him really come out of his shell.

*You can learn this phrase and many more in my other book: 500 Really Useful English Phrases.

Vocabulary and Phrases:

To be introverted: to have an inward personality. To not like speaking to people and being in social situations.

Example 1: He's such an introvert, he never speaks to anyone he doesn't know.

Example 2: My husband is very introverted, he hates parties and mixing with other people.

To be modest: to not talk too much about your achievements. To not speak about yourself all the time.

Example: Even though she is very successful, she is modest about her achievements.

A domineering (personality): to be dominating. To try to put people below you.

Example: Her husband had a really domineering personality, so she was always scared to say her opinion.

To come out of one's shell: to stop being shy. To start to be more open and sociable.

Example: She has really started to come out of her shell since she started doing acting lessons.

Part Four

My maths class after that is a little frustrating. My teacher is a sweetheart, but she can be such a pushover, letting students like Allison hand in work late. I'm a driven student and can't stand to see a teacher that's so submissive. She's still a really affable teacher though. I would talk with her all day if I could. She is always so positive and supportive. That motivation gets me through the rest of my day.

Vocabulary and Phrases:

A sweetheart: a really nice, sweet person.

Example: She's such a sweetheart, she's always offering to help with everything.

A pushover: a weak person that can be easy convinced to do something.

Example: My husband is such a pushover, he lets our daughter do whatever she likes.

To be driven/to have a driven personality: to be single minded and keep going until you get what you want.

Example: He's pretty driven. That's how he has managed to become so successful.

To be submissive: to never take the lead. To always be a follower.

Example: Some women like submissive husbands, but I would get a bit annoyed if my husband always did what I said.

To be affable: To be likeable.

Example: He’s a pretty affable guy. So he’s always done well as a salesman.

Extra Vocabulary and Phrases

To be hard work: this phrase describes someone who has a difficult personality.

Example: My ex-wife was quite hard work. She was always complaining about everything.

Note: This is different from 'hard working'.

Passive: to not be aggressive:

Example: He's too passive. He needs to be stronger and not let people push him around.

To be astute: to be a very quick thinker. To see the connections between things. To have a sharp mind.

Example: He's very astute so he realised that his wife was having an affair pretty quickly.

To be good natured: to have a nice, soft personality.

Example: He's always been good natured ever since he was a baby.

FASHION

PART ONE

In attitude and fashion, I was a tomboy up until the day I met Tom. He was my boss and the most fashionable man I have ever met. I walked into the workplace in baggy jeans without thinking my first day, and he pulled me aside to say, "Hey, do you even see what you're wearing? Are you not even trying to look good?" I was offended and shook him off, but he confronted me every morning until he finally came in with a box of clothes. "Here, this is what's trendy right now. I know this is a casual workplace, but let's make the clothes smart casual, alright?"

"Did you buy these? You really didn't have to-" I said. He replied, "I got them all on-sale. Ooh, look at this blouse here. Isn't it stylish? These colours are really in this season."

"It's ugly," I said bluntly, looking at the piece of clothing he was holding.

"I'm so sorry to hear you have no sense of style. I think we need to come up with a better 'look' for you. We shouldn't abandon your personal preferences completely, but let's try to match it with what's in fashion."

Vocabulary and Phrases:

A tomboy: this is a girl who both dresses and behaves a little like a boy.

Example: She was such a tomboy when she was younger but now she is a famous fashion model.

Fashionable: to wear clothes that look good and are the current popular fashion.

Example: The good thing about wearing black is that it is always fashionable.

Baggy (clothes): very loose clothes.

Example: I don't like that shirt, it's a bit too baggy.

Trendy: this means that something (someone) is fashionable.

Example: She's so trendy. She always wears the most fashionable clothes.

Smart casual: 'casual' clothes are just regular clothes that you would wear outside of work. 'Smart casual' is nicer than that but not as formal as a suit etc.

Example: Most employees in this company wear smart casual but others still like to wear a suit to work.

To be on-sale: this is when something is a cheaper price than usual.

Example: I like to shop at new year because everything is on-sale.

To be stylish: to have a good style. To wear nice clothes.

Example: It's weird because my mother is actually a lot more stylish than me.

To be 'in': This means that something is popular right now.

Example: I hear that bright colours are really 'in' at the moment.

This season/last season/next season: clothes are released in connection to the season. So they speak about fashion in 'seasons'.

Example: Light cotton shirts are really popular this season.

A sense of style: a good feeling for fashion.

Note: 'style' is not always about fashion but also your actions and behavior.

Example: I've never really had any real sense of style.

A 'look': this is the general atmosphere of what you wear.

Example: I don't really like this 'look', I find dark colours a bit boring.

To be 'in fashion': to be popular right now.

Example: I don't care if they're in fashion, there's no way that I'm wearing sandals!

Tom was right that I had no fashion sense. Still, thanks to him I learned over time how to choose clothes that looked good on me. He was really helpful, and the two of us stayed friends even after the business closed. I still think it's only thanks to his fashion advice that I got as many interviews as I did when I went to look for more work. Who could've known the kind of impact a box of clothes would have?

Vocabulary and Phrases:

Fashion sense: your feeling and understanding of clothes and fashion. Good fashion sense is when your clothes look good. Bad fashion sense is when your clothes look bad.

Example: She's got a strange fashion sense, but somehow she always looks ok.

Youtube Fashion Channels:

Niomi Smart

Fashion Rocks my Socks

Fashion Channel

GOSSIP

PART ONE

My least favourite part of the day has always been lunch. From school to my office job, people seem to think the cafeteria is the place to be to talk about other people behind their backs. It's especially frustrating when they're talking about someone I know, like Lindsay. She's always had problems with people spreading rumours about her. They were so two-faced; they'd speak nicely to her face then say bad things about her when she wasn't there. With those back stabbers, you never know where you stand with them.

Vocabulary and Phrases:

To talk about someone behind their back: to say bad things about someone when they are not around to defend themselves.

Example: I never tell Jane anything personal. I know she talks about people behind their backs so I'm very careful around her.

To spread a rumour: to tell lots of people a (possibly true/untrue) secret about someone else.

Example: I heard that she has been spreading rumours about me.

To be two faced: to be nice to someone when you see them, but then say bad things about them when they are not around.

Example: She's so two faced. She's so polite to me but then goes straight to my other friends and starts gossiping about me.

A back stabber/back stabbing: somebody who betrays you. To say bad things about someone when they are not there.

Example 1: He is such a back stabber. He told my boss about the mistake I made.

Example 2: I hated that job. There was too much back stabbing going on, you could never relax and just do your work.

You don't know where you stand with them: you don't feel comfortable around this person because you don't know what they are thinking.

Example: One minute she's happy and the next she is angry. You just don't know where you stand with her, it's totally exhausting.

Note: the positive version of this is 'you know where you stand with them'.

Part Two

I was in the office cafeteria one day to get lunch when I heard someone in the back room. "Did you hear about that thing with Lindsay's friend?" he said.

"What?!!... Are they talking about me?" I said under my breath and stormed into the conference room. It turned out to be David. He was always changing who he was picking on like a fickle child. I couldn't believe how he could talk about me when I was just in the other room! "Are you trying to stir up trouble?" I asked after entering.

"What? No, we were talking about your promotion. Congratulations."

I blushed at the misunderstanding. "Oh, uh... Thank you. Sorry about that." I said.

Vocabulary and Phrases:

Did you hear about....?: This is a question people use when they start gossiping about something.

Example: Did you hear about Tom? Apparently he quit his job and has run away with a woman twice his age!

To pick on someone: to bully someone.

Example: Why are you always picking on me? I’ve never done anything to you.

To be fickle: to change your opinion/tastes etc easily.

Example: He's so fickle, first he says he loves Julie and then he says he loves Helen. He just changes his mind every 5 minutes.

To stir up trouble: to say things that will cause problems.

Example: I didn't want to stir up trouble so I didn't tell her that I saw her underage son drinking alcohol.

If you want to learn how to gossip, the only show you need to watch is 'Made in Chelsea'. All they do for the whole show is gossip about each other.

HEALTH

Personally, I think it's important to take care of yourself. It's not as hard as it seems to watch what you eat or at least try to lead a balanced lifestyle. I always appreciate it when I see someone who's in shape, even if they're not the same picture of health that I am now. Of course, I wasn't always this way. My health now is all thanks to my personal trainer, Jaime.

Vocabulary and Phrases:

To take care of oneself: To be careful to maintain a good physical condition.

Example: It's important to look after yourself as you get older.

To watch what you eat: to be careful about the foods you eat.

Example: I never used to watch what I ate, but now I do as I seem to get fat a lot easier.

To lead a balanced lifestyle: to take care of yourself. To exercise and to eat well.

Example: The key to health is to lead a balanced lifestyle.

To be in shape/to be out of shape: to be fit/unfit. To have a healthy body

Example: I was in shape before I started this job, but now I'm totally out of shape.

A picture of health: this phrase means that you look really healthy.

Example: Ever since he changed his diet, he's been the picture of health.

Personal Trainer: a person who designs an exercise and diet programme to get you in shape. They also supervise your exercise.
Example: It's good to hire a personal trainer because they force you to exercise.

PART TWO

I realized I had been feeling poorly and wanted to be fit, so I signed up for a gym membership. Jaime was the trainer that came with it. The first time he saw me, he said, "I'm going to make you fit as a fiddle, Sir." I laughed at the time, but it's true. He put me on a fitness regime. Later on, he kick-started my metabolism with health foods and taught me all about alternative medicine.

Vocabulary and Phrases:

To feel poorly: to feel a little unwell.

Example: I felt a bit poorly so I went home early.

To be fit: To have a healthy body. To be able to do physical activities easily.

Example: He's pretty fit for his age. He still goes swimming every day.

To be fit as a fiddle: this phrase means that you are in excellent physical condition.

Example: I'm 80 years old and still fit as a fiddle.

A fitness regime: A physical activity programme designed to keep you fit.

Example: My new fitness regime involves exercising everyday for 30 minutes before breakfast.

Metabolism: how well/quickly your body uses (burns) energy.

Example: I've always had a pretty slow metabolism so I put weight on easily.

Health foods: foods that actively promote good health.

Example: The problem with health foods is that they are often quite expensive.

Alternative medicine: Medicines and practices which are not based on the standard western techniques.

Example: I have had a lot of success using alternative medicines for curing my hay fever.

He even gave me diet tips for my wife. She's always been lactose intolerant and could only eat gluten free foods. I applied his tips at home and found that both of us began to get very healthy. His exercises also raised my endurance enough that I got back into long distance running. I couldn't have done it without him.

Vocabulary and Phrases:

To be (lactose etc) intolerant: to be allergic to (milk etc).

Example: He's lactose intolerant so make sure that you don't put milk in his tea.

Gluten free (food): foods that don't contain wheat or other sources of gluten.

Example: This gluten free diet is great for losing weight. But it is difficult to avoid wheat as it seems to be in everything.

Endurance: the ability to keep going. To continue on.

Example: Some of those athletes have amazing endurance.

Health youtube channels.

Here are two popular youtube channels. Both are about health and healthy eating.

The Life Regenerator.

Freelea the Bannana Girl (Warning: sometimes contains swear words).

COMPUTERS

PART ONE

Computers are amazingly helpful but when they go wrong they can completely mess people up. Nowadays it seems that people can't do anything without computers. If the computer stops functioning then we can't function. We have become completely dependent on them. I came to realize just how much we depend on computers when I was working at a local company last year. The computer I was working on needed some new software. I think it was an upgrade to the operating system or something. Everything was going fine and then suddenly the image on the monitor started going crazy.

Vocabulary and Phrases.

Software: These are programmes that you can install onto your computer to perform certain functions. For example if you wanted to make a video, you would install 'video making software' onto your computer.

Example: *I like to run Linux on my computer because a lot of the software is actually free.*

An upgrade: This is when you make improvements to your computer or install a newer or better piece of software on your computer.

Example 1: *I decided to get my computer's memory upgraded.*

Example 2: *This piece of software comes with free yearly upgrades.*

Operating system (OS): This is the main software on a computer. It acts as an in-between software between the hardware and any program you may run on your computer. For example 'Microsoft Windows OS'.

Example 1: *My operating system is pretty old so I can't run a lot of the new software that is coming out nowadays.*

Example 2: *I love this OS because it never crashes*.*

*if a computer 'crashes' this means that it stops working. This is usually related to the OS/software rather than the hardware.

A monitor: If you have a desktop computer then the 'monitor' is the device with the screen on the front.

Example: *I need to replace my monitor because the screen is cracked.*

At first I just thought there was a problem with the software. But then because all of the computers in the office were networked they all started to go wrong as well. At this point I really started panicking. What had I done? Had I just broken every computer in the office? To make matters worse I hadn't actually backed up any of my work so that would all be lost too. After a while I calmed down and called tech support. They talked me through all of the possible problems and got me to reboot the computers. They wanted to email me a patch to see if that would fix the problem but the Wi-Fi router wasn't working either. They even got me to check the computer hardware and all of the USB ports, but I couldn't find anything wrong. In the end we decided that it was probably a computer virus and that a computer specialist should come in to fix it. But the next day when they arrived all of the computers were magically working again. It was a complete mystery, they just seemed to fix themselves overnight. Of course now I'm very careful to back up my files and I absolutely never update my computer software!

Vocabulary and Phrases:

Network(ed) (computers): If your computers are 'networked' that means they are connected to each other. Therefore they can all access the same files and information.

Example: *All of the computers at my work are networked, so if one of them gets a virus, then they are all at risk.*

To back-up files: This means to make copies of the files that are on your computer. So you have the file on your computer and back-ups on disk etc.

Example 1: *Make sure to back up all of your files, just in case something happens to your computer.*

Example 2: *I make backups of all of my files every evening.*

Technical support: This means 'help with technical issues you may have with your computer'. This is a service that companies often offer.

Example 1: *I choose that computer because the support is supposed to be excellent.*

Example 2: *I hate ringing for technical support. They just speak in jargon, and I have no idea what they are talking about.*

To reboot (a computer): This is when you have a problem with the software (often the operating system) and need to start the computer again so that the problem doesn't occur again.

Example: *If you have any problems, just reboot your computer and that should sort it all out.*

A patch: This is something that you install onto your computer to fix or improve a certain piece of software. Software companies often make these when they discover slight problems in their product.

Example 1: *Please install this patch if you have an earlier version of this software.*

Example 2: *This security patch will make it impossible for your personal details to be stolen.*

A Wi-Fi router: This is a device that allows you to have wi-fi internet access in your house etc.

Example: *That router is pretty good. I can get wi-fi coverage throughout my house.*

Hardware: This is the actual physical equipment within the computer. For example a CD drive is a piece of hardware.

Example: *This computer comes with some excellent hardware including a very powerful graphics card.*

USB port: This is a type of socket where you can plug in things like an external disk drive or a mouse*.

*A mouse is a device you use to move the cursor (pointer) around on the computer screen.

Example: *Just plug the disk drive into the USB socket (port).*

A computer virus: This is a programme that will cause problems on your computer. Your computer can be affected by them if you visit certain websites or open an email that contains one of them.

Example: *Make sure that you never open an email from someone you don't know as it may contain a computer virus.*

MORE USEFUL WORDS:

To run (software): If you 'run' software on your computer, that means that software is on your computer. You have installed and can use that software on your computer.

Example 1: *I run 'windows' on my computer.*

Example 2: *You need to enter the security key before that software will run properly.*

Memory: Computers have two types of memory. Hard drive memory is how much data you can store on your computer. RAM is how much data a computer can process at one time.

Example 1: *This computer has a lot of memory so you should be able to store a lot of data without too much trouble.*

Example 2: *There's not much RAM on this computer so its impossible to watch movies or play games on it.*

A driver: This is a piece of software that helps connect your computer with an outside piece of hardware such as a printer.

Example: *If you want to download photos from your camera to your computer you will need to install a special driver.*

Computer Youtube Channels:

Eli The Computer Guy.

Cnet.

Computer World.

PETS

Note: Most of these words relate to dogs.

PART ONE

Have you ever been absolutely and completely against doing something and then when you finally do it you love it? This happened to me when I first got a dog. Now don't get me wrong I don't hate dogs, it's just that I've never really been that interested in animals. If a dog ran up to my family in the park I would be the only one that it would ignore. It would visit everyone else and then just walk right by me as if I didn't exist. Anyway for some reason my wife decided that she absolutely must get a dog. We had lots of arguments about it but eventually I just gave up. I did however insist that she would have to research all of the breeds and choose one that was easy to train and socialize. I also insisted that she would have to take care of all of the training and grooming once we got it.

Vocabulary and Phrases:

Breeds/to breed: 'A breed' of animal is a 'type' of animal. For example a 'Yorkshire terrier' is a breed of dog. 'To breed' an animal means to professionally produce pets for sale.

Example: *There are so many different breeds of dogs, that it's easy to find one that suits your personality.*

Example 2: *I got my puppy from a well known breeder. You should always do your research when buying a pet.*

Training: This is when you work with your pet to develop good behavior.

Example 1: *My dog is pretty well trained, but she does bark quite a lot.*

Example 2: *Training a pet is something you have to keep doing. If you stop doing it, the pet may go back to its bad habits.*

Socialization: This is when you train your pet to be good around people or other animals.

Example 1: *Socialization is so important when keeping a pet. You need them to be well behaved around other people and animals.*

Example 2: *You should make sure that your pet is properly socialized so that it doesn't suddenly bite someone or attack another animal.*

Grooming: This is when you take care of your pet's appearance. You keep it clean and brush it's coat.

Example 1: *People absolutely love their pets in England so grooming is actually quite big business.*

Example 2: *I like to make sure that my dog is well groomed.*

Well, after months of careful research she decided on getting a dachshund. Not because they are easy to train (they're not!), but because they are cute. I was already seriously regretting this decision. I don't know much but I felt that deciding on a breed due to its 'cuteness level' would probably end in disaster. Anyway, she found a lady nearby whose dogs had recently had a litter and we went along to see if any of them would be appropriate for us. When we arrived there were 4 puppies left. It was quite funny because one of them kept on running off and investigating everything. Even though I was still completely against the idea of getting a dog I found this particular puppy to be pretty funny. My wife liked all of them but as soon as I picked up this particular one *it was love*. We seemed to have an instant rapport. That was it, I insisted that we *must* get that one! On the drive home I thought 'what just happened'? I went from being totally against the whole idea to insisting that we buy it in about 2 minutes!

Vocabulary and Phrases:

A litter: When dogs have children there are usually quite a lot of them. This group of puppies is called 'a litter'.

Example: *My dog had a large litter of puppies. We ended up keeping most of them though!*

Rapport: This describes having a good relationship with someone or a pet. There is a good feeling between the two parties. You understand each other.

Example: *It took quite a long time to get a good rapport with my dog but we have a good relationship now.*

When we got home my wife stuck to her promise of looking after and training our new puppy. There was just one problem, dachshunds (or 'daxis') are seriously hard to train. They just seem to do what they want to do. If you through a sick they might retrieve it but there's no way they will return it back to you. When you let them off the lead when you are in the park there is no chance you will get them to sit patiently when you want to put the lead back on. And if you have to flea them they will wriggle and make it impossible to do. After a while my wife was starting to look a bit panicked! "How on earth am I going to train this naughty little thing?" Eventually we discovered 'positive reinforcement'. This is where you give the puppy a tread every time they do as you ask. This worked pretty well but our dog is still very stubborn. Anyway at least she's cute! Right?

Vocabulary and Phrases:

To retrieve: If you throw a stick or something and your dog gets it and brings it back to you then it has 'retrieved it'.

Example: *Hunters often use dogs to retrieve the animals they have shot.*

Lead/Leash: This is piece of cord or string that you attach to your dog's collar to keep them under control. You hold one end of the string and connect the other end to the collar.

Example 1: *In that park, dogs must be kept on a leash at all times.*

Example 2: *When we go down to the beach I let my dog off of the lead so she can have a good run around and have a swim.*

To flea: This is when you give your pet some medicine to make sure that they don't get fleas.

Example: *It's important to make sure that you flea your dog every 3 months.*

Positive reinforcement: This is a pet training technique where you reward good behavior. This means that your pet is more likely to do the things that you want it to do because it knows that it will get rewarded for it.

Example: *I think that using positive reinforcement is the easiest way to train a dog.*

Pets Youtube Channels:

The Pet Collective.

Dog TV.

PetsTV.

MUSIC

PART ONE

When I tell people that I'm a professional musician, they immediately think that I'm either a classical musician or that I'm in a famous band. Actually I'm a songwriter and session musician. That means that I basically have two jobs. One is to write lyrics for other people's songs and the other is to play the music on other people's records. I didn't start like this though. Like a lot of aspiring musicians I started in a band hoping to famous.

Vocabulary and Phrases:

A session musician: This is a professional musician who is hired to play on other people's records. For example a singer that isn't in a band would hire session musicians to provide the music on their albums or to play in the backing band when they play live.

Example: *Although session musicians never become famous, it is an easier way to make a regular income than trying to become a famous musician.*

Lyrics: These are the words to a song. A 'lyricist' is someone who writes song lyrics.

Example 1: *I don't like dance music. I prefer to listen to the lyrics of a song rather than to just dance around to it.*

Example 2: *I think Bob Dylan is my favorite lyricist of all time.*

An aspiring musician: Someone who is trying to be a professional musician.

Example: *Like most aspiring musicians, I have a part-time job to help me get by.*

My band was a type of fusion between indie and blues music. We played some acoustic stuff, but mostly it was pretty loud electric guitar type music. We started by doing small gigs in our local area. While we were doing that we also sent off hundreds of demo tapes to various record labels. Most of them weren't interested but after a few years of pushing we were finally signed to quite a small label. Even though it was a small record label we were convinced that we would have a top ten hit on the charts and all be rich and famous. The reality was that even though we had a record deal, that didn't actually mean that we would automatically become popular. In fact we never became popular at all!

Vocabulary and Phrases:

Fusion: This is music that mixes two or more types of music. For example some bands mix 'rap' with 'rock music'.

Example: *Fusion bands used to be more popular than they are now.*

Indie music: Originally this referred to music from 'independent record labels' (small record companies). But now it refers to a type of 'alternative' rock music. A famous indie band is 'The Stone Roses'.

Example: *I used to listen to indie music when I was younger but now I prefer more mainstream stuff.*

The blues (blues music): This is a type of music that originated from African-American culture. It often consists of guitar and singing. It is often quite sad.

Example 1: *I think that John Lee Hooker and BB King are the most famous blues musicians in the world.*

Example 2: *If you are feeling sad then probably the best music to listen to is the blues. It will match your mood perfectly.*

Acoustic: This is music that is played on non-electric instruments. Therefore an 'acoustic guitar' is one that you do not plug into an amplifier.

Example 1: *I love acoustic music, it's so relaxing.*

Example 2: *My neighbor plays an acoustic guitar. I'm glad it's not an electric one as I think that would be too loud.*

Example 3: *Semi-acoustic guitars are pretty popular because you get the same sound but you can amplify them easily as well.*

A gig: This is a live music show. For example if a band plays a 'gig', that means that they have played a 'show'. If they are 'gigging' that means that they are playing lots of different shows.

Example 1: *I saw an amazing gig last night.*

Example 2: *They started off just gigging at local pubs and then gradually got a following. Now they are pretty famous in the UK.*

A demo (tape): This is a recording that you send to record labels or music venues to make them interested in signing you (record label) or having you play a show (venue).

Example: *If you are just starting out, I really recommend that you get a demo tape as soon as possible.*

A record label: This is a company that releases the music of various different artists.

Example: *That label usually just releases hip hop records.*

To be signed (to a record label): This is when a singer/band has a contract with a record label to make and release records. If an artist is 'unsigned' then that means that they are not connected to a record label.

Example 1: *She got signed as soon as she left school.*

Example 2: *A lot of unsigned bands are just releasing their music on their own over the internet.*

A top ten hit: This is a song that is one of the ten most popular songs on the chart in a certain week.

Example: *That song was a top ten hit on both the US and the UK charts.*

The charts: This is a record* of how well songs have sold in a certain week. Who has the most popular song/album that week.

*Here we mean 'record' as in 'list', not as in 'music record'.

Example: *I don't follow the charts. Most of the music on there is pretty awful to tell you the truth.*

A record deal: This means that a musician/band has a contract with a record label to release records. They have been signed by a record label.

Example: *The day I got a record deal was the happiest day of my life.*

We did release one album but it didn't really sell very well. In fact it sold quite badly. Even so, we did have one great experience. We were asked by a popular band on the same label as us to go on tour with them. They were the headline act and we opened for them. It was an amazing experience playing in front of so many people. But even though we were finally playing in front of big audiences, they weren't actually *our* fans and we still didn't sell many records. Eventually we decided to break up. The funny thing was, our vocalist decided to go solo and is now very successful. In fact he eventually hired me as a session musician to play on his records!

Vocabulary and Phrases:

To go on tour: This is when a musician/band travels around playing shows in different towns/countries.

Example: *I hope they go on tour again. I missed them the last time they were in London.*

To headline/a headline act: This is when a singer/band is the main act of a show. They usually play at the end.

Example 1: *Who's headlining at the festival this year?*

Example 2: *I thought the opening act was actually better than the headlining act.*

To open for (another band): This is when a smaller, less known band plays before a more famous band in a concert/show.

Example: *Last year they were opening for ABC Band and now they are the main act.*

Vocals/a vocalist: 'Vocals' refers to 'singing'. So a 'vocalist' is a singer.

Example 1: *I love the vocals on that song.*

Example 2: *She's not a very good vocalist, but her lyrics are amazing. I think most people buy her stuff to listen to the words rather than her voice.*

A solo artist: This is a musician/singer that makes music on their own. They are not in a band.

Example 1: *I think that she is my favorite solo artist. I love her voice.*

Example 2: *He was in a band but eventually he went solo.*

More Useful Words:

Funky: This is an adjective to describe music that has a good beat. It is often used to describe music that you would want to dance to.

Example: *I love that song, it's so funky.*

Instrumental: This is music that doesn't feature any vocals/singing. Music made with only instruments.

Example: *As I get older I prefer instrumental music. I find listening to lyrics a bit distracting.*

A solo: This is when a musician in a band plays over the rhythm of the song. It is often done by playing single notes rather than chords.

Example 1: *Jimi Hendrix was amazing at guitar solos.*

Example 2: *I don't like heavy metal, there are too many solos.*

Unplugged: This describes an album or concert that was recorded/played acoustically. They did not use electric instruments.

Example 1: *I like their usual records but I loved their 'unplugged' album as well.*

Example 2: *I heard that they are doing an unplugged concert later this month.*

A chord: This is a collection of notes all played at the same time.

Example: *A lot of the most popular songs only ever really use 3 or 4 chords. That proves that music doesn't have to be complicated to be good.*

Acapella: This is singing without any instruments.

Example: *Recently 'acapella bands' are becoming more and more popular. I think it's because they can just upload their songs onto Youtube. They don't have to sign to a record label to get their music out there.*

Music Youtube Channel:

The following is a music review channel so you can learn how to talk about music.

The Needle Drop.

Books

Part One

The older you get the more you tend to think back to your past. You start to become more nostalgic. Lots of people just look through their old photos and remember that way. I like to look through my bookshelf as each book that I bought holds certain memories for me. Each one represents a different period in my life. When I flick through the pages or just read the blub I can clearly remember how I was feeling when I first read the book.

Vocabulary and Phrases:

A blurb: This is the description at the back of a book.

Example: I always read a book's blurb before I buy it.

I really started getting into books when I was a teenager. I absolutely loved romance <u>bestsellers</u>. You know the ones that I mean. They are usually <u>paperbacks</u> and probably written by people using <u>pen names</u>. I adored all of the complicated love stories and found them completely <u>unputdownable</u>. My mother always says that if I had spent as much time on my studies as I did reading those books I would have done a lot better in school.

<u>Vocabulary and Phrases:</u>

A bestseller: This is a book that has sold very well in it's genre.

Example 1: *That book was a surprise bestseller.*

Example 2: *He is a famous bestselling author.*

A paperback/hardback: These are the soft and hard cover versions of a book.

Example: *I prefer paperbacks to hardbacks. They may be easier to break but they are also cheaper and not so heavy to carry.*

A pen name: This is a name authors use other than their real name. Some people publish their books under a different name than their real name.

Example: *I write in two different genres so I use different pen names for each one.*

Unputdownable: This describes a book that is so good that you can't stop reading it.

Note: you may not find this word in your dictionary as it is a very casual and 'new' word.

Example: *I find her books completely unputdownable. They are great for taking on holiday because you need enough time to really get into them.*

Then there are all of the heavy, serious hardback books from my university days. Of course they are all very academic and full of references, glossaries, and indices. All totally boring. Although I like to think back to my time at university, I hate looking at these books. For this period of my life I'd rather look at photos!

Vocabulary and Phrases:

References: If a book mentions information or a quote from somewhere else, they 'reference' it.

Example: *I don't like non-fiction that doesn't use references. How can I believe what they are saying if they don't offer proof. It just looks like opinion then.*

An index: This is a list at the end of a book that lists all of the important 'key words' or 'key points' from a book. For example, if you have a diet book but you want to know specifically about what to eat while pregnant, then you would check under 'pregnancy' in the index and find all the times 'pregnancy' has been mentioned in the book.

Example: *Having an index is especially important in non-fiction. Fiction books don't really need them.*

A glossary: This is a list that explains the difficult/specialist words in a book or text. For example in the book you are reading now there is a short text and then a glossary explaining the words used. You are reading a glossary right now!

Example: *It's important to have a glossary at the end of a book. Especially if the book uses lots of jargon or really special language.*

After I left university I got really into classic literature. Of course I bought the occasional book by a debut author, but mostly I just read the old classics. After I got my first job I spent a lot of money on buying the collected works (unabridged of course!) of some of my favorite authors. I also managed to get a few first editions and signed copies of some of the books.

Vocabulary and Phrases:

A début book/author: *A 'debut book' is an author's first book. A 'debut author' is an author that has just published their first book.*

Example: I like her debut novel, but everything since then has been a little boring.

The collected works (of an author): This is a set (that you can buy) of all of an author's books.

Example: *I bought the collected works of Shakespeare, but it was pretty expensive.*

Unabridged: This is a book that has not been shortened or altered in any way.

Example: *Even though it is much more difficult to understand I totally prefer the unabridged version.*

A first edition: This is the 'first print' of a book. Paper books are printed in 'editions'. If the book is popular then having a 'first edition' can be a collector's item. For example a first edition of 'War and Peace' would cost quite a lot of money.

Example: *My brother is a real book enthusiast, he always wants the first edition of books.*

A signed copy (of a book): This is a book that has been signed (autographed) by the author that wrote it.

Example: *I went and met the author and got a signed copy of his book.*

More recently I've really gotten into biographies and autobiographies. Although I suspect that lots of autobiographies nowadays are written by ghostwriters I still like to read about other people's lives. Another thing that I enjoy are audio books, but I tend to leave them in my car rather than on my bookshelf. Anyway, it's fun to travel through your past by looking at books, I highly recommend you do it some time.

Vocabulary and Phrases:

A biography: A book written about somebody else's life.

Example: *I generally prefer autobiographies but the biography of Winston Churchill was pretty interesting.*

An autobiography: A book written by someone about their own life.

Example: *His autobiography was absolutely amazing. He's led such an interesting life.*

A ghostwriter: This is someone who writes books for other people. For example if a footballer wants to write an autobiography but they don't have the writing skills then they would hire a ghostwriter to write it for them.

Example: *I have been a ghostwriter for years. Actually I have written the autobiography of some really famous people.*

An audio book: This is a recording of a book. So you can listen to the book rather than read it.

Example: *Non-fiction audio books are great for the car. You can learn something as you commute to work.*

Books Youtube channels:

The Readables.

Books and Quills.

Appearance

Have you ever heard the phrase 'never judge a book by its cover'? Basically it means that you should never judge people, things and situations based on appearance alone. I'm sure you'd agree that this is very good advice. But do you actually do it? Most people would say that they never judge other people based on their looks and appearance. But I don't believe this for a second. For example I saw a rather portly gentleman this morning and the first thing I thought was 'that's a pretty big beer belly he must be a bit of a drinker'. Now of course I don't know this man and have no right to judge, but I did it before I could stop myself. Be honest for a second, do you treat very striking or classically beautiful people different from someone who is quite plain? Would you speak differently to someone who is very glamorous than to someone who was quite elegant? Maybe you treat everyone the same but I'm betting that you are in the minority.

Vocabulary and Phrases:

Never judge a book by its cover: This phrase means that you should never judge people, situations or things by their appearances alone.

Example: *Even though he was very polite and well dressed, it turned out that he was a wanted criminal. That goes to show 'you should never judge a book by its cover'.*

To be portly: This describes a man that is quite chubby. A bit overweight. It is not a very common word, but you will still hear it sometimes.

Example: *He's always been a bit portly, but recently he's put on even more weight and he looks pretty unhealthy.*

A beer belly: This describes the fat stomach of someone (usually male) that drinks a lot. Sometimes they look quite slim but just have a big belly.

Example: *My husband decided to cut back on alcohol because he was getting a huge beer belly.*

Striking: This describes someone who looks quite unusual. They catch your eye. They stand out. Perhaps they are particularly good looking or have strong features. This is usually a positive thing to say about someone.

Example 1: *She has lots of black curly hair and bright green eyes. She's quite striking actually.*

Example 2: *She looks very striking in that lovely red dress.*

To be classically beautiful/handsome: This describes someone that has standard good looks. Most people would say that this person is good looking. It's not really a matter of opinion.

Example: *My husband is quite classically handsome.*

Plain: This describes someone (usually female) whose appearance is neither good looking or ugly. They are unremarkable looking.

Example: *She's not ugly, she's just a bit plain looking.*

Glamorous: This describes someone (usually female) who has a colorful or showy appearance. They like clothes, make-up and jewelry that makes them stand out.

Example: *My mother is actually even more glamorous than I am. It was really embarrassing when I was younger.*

Elegant: This describe someone who holds themselves very well. They are polite and refined.

Example: *You look very elegant in that dress.*

LANGUAGES

PART ONE

Usually when I tell people that I'm interested in languages they say "oh I could never learn another language" or " I'm terrible with languages". But is that actually true? I mean, ok, maybe they'll never be bilingual or a polyglot, but I bet that with a little effort they could get by in another language. It actually doesn't take that much to be able to make yourself understood in another language. I'm sure that if they just made an effort they would pick up the basics quite easily.

Vocabulary and Phrases:

Bilingual: To be able to speak two languages fluently.

Example: *If your partner speaks a different language from your native one then it is easier to ensure that your children grow up being bilingual.*

Polyglot: This is someone who speaks a lot of languages. Usually three or more.

Example: *A friend of mind is a polyglot. I don't know why but she picks up languages really easily.*

(To be able) to get by (in a language): This phrase refers to when you can survive in a country with your knowledge of that language.

You are not fluent but you can survive on holiday using your language skills.

Example: *I can get by in French when I'm on holiday, but I'd have trouble living there.*

To make yourself understood: This is when you can't really speak a language properly, but you know enough to be able to communicate what you want to people.

Example: *My Spanish grammar is absolutely terrible but I know enough words to make myself understood.*

To pick up languages: This means to learn new languages or words naturally/easily.

Example: *I find that the easiest way to pick up languages is to just watch a lot of TV. After a while you just start understanding naturally.*

Usually when we talk about language acquisition we think about 'learning foreign languages'. But actually we are all acquiring new language all the time. I mean think about it for a second, you probably learnt a new word recently without even noticing it. Every workplace has its own different jargon that it uses. When you started working there you probably had no idea what everyone else was saying, but after a few months you were speaking the same lingo as everyone else. You just learnt it naturally. Also you probably hear new slang all the time either on TV or on the street. Actually in some areas there is so much slang that it's almost like a totally different dialect. Of course you didn't study this slang, but just by hearing it around you learnt it naturally.

Vocabulary and Phrases:

Language acquisition/ to acquire (a language): This is when you learn a new language.

Example 1: *I find it pretty easy to acquire new languages.*

Example 2: *Most people think that language acquisition is easy for children, but I don't think that is true. I think that getting the pronunciation correct is probably easier for them though.*

Jargon: This is industry specific language. It often refers to language that is confusing to people who are not familiar with that topic.

Example: *When I first started getting interested in finance the jargon really confused me. But after a while I just sort of naturally learnt it all.*

Lingo: This is a very casual word which refers to local (dialect) or specialized language. It can also refer to foreign languages.

Example 1: *Every job has its own industry specific language. However it only usually takes about a month or two to learn the lingo and then everything should be fine.*

Example 2: *When I moved to Japan it only took about a year to learn the lingo. But learning to read and write took a lot longer than that.*

Slang: This is very casual language. It is often more frequently used by younger people.

Example: *If you plan to actually live in a foreign country then it is important to learn some of the local slang.*

Dialect: This is local language. Sometimes it is completely different from the country's main language and sometimes it is just different words for specific things.

Example 1: *The problem with learning a few phrases for traveling around India is that there are so many dialects that it's impossible to know whether they would understand you. The good thing is that most people can speak English there.*

Example 2: *In the Kansai region of Japan they speak a dialect called Kansai-Ben.*

Language Youtube channels:

Fluent in 3 months.

Lindsey Does Languages.

Employment

Part One

Ever since I was young I have never been that interested in having a normal career. Actually all I ever really wanted to do was to go travelling. When I left school, most of my friends went off to do vocations such as being teachers or doctors but I took a very different path. I decided that what I would do was to travel around the world while working in different jobs to pay for it. I ended up travelling for over 5 years and had a lot of different jobs over that time. Some had pretty good salaries but most were minimum wage. There were also a few 9-5 regular jobs but a lot of them were temporary and had no job security. I didn't mind too much though, because I was just working so that I could live in that country not because I particularly loved the job. I wasn't too bothered how I made a living. If it was easy, not dangerous and made me a livelihood then I was happy.

Vocabulary and Phrases:

Career: This refers to your working life and the path you take in your professional life. For example if you have mostly worked in 'education' you would say that your career has been in 'education'.

Example 1: *Throughout my career I have always tried to do my best.*

Example 2: *Early in my career in sales I knew that I wanted to start my own sales company.*

Example 3: *At the age of 40 I decided to have a career change and became an interpreter.*

A vocation: This is a job that you are totally suited for. You are naturally good at this job.

Example 1: *I always liked working with kids so I really felt that being a teacher was more than just a job for me, it was a vocation.*

Example 2: *Becoming a doctor is so difficult. Therefore it's easier if you see it as your vocation rather than just a job.*

Salary: This is the money you get paid for working in a job. It often refers to the total amount you get during the year.

Example: I like this job but the salary is pretty low.

Minimum wage: This is a wage set by the government that is the lowest you can get paid at a job. A 'minimum wage job' is a badly paid job.

Example 1: *The first job I ever had, I got paid the minimum wage.*

Example 2: *There are only minimum wage jobs where I live, so I decided to start my own company instead.*

A nine to five job: This refers to a regular full-time job where you work from Monday to Friday, from 9am to 5pm.

Example: *After years of being self employed, I don't think that I could work at a nine to five job anymore.*

Job security: This refers to how difficult it is to lose your job. If you don't have a contract then you probably don't have very good 'job security'. If you are in a stable job then there is a good chance that you have good 'job security'.

Example: *The problem nowadays is that there is no real job security. There is no such thing as a job for life now.*

To make a living: To make money to live.

Example: *I used to make a living by buying things and then selling them on Ebay for a profit.*

A livelihood: This is how you make a living. How you make money.

Example: *The problem with making your livelihood from tourism is that it's really difficult to make money during the winter.*

Part Two

One of the first jobs that I had was working in a restaurant in Australia. It was basically a part-time job where I had to work the lunch shift one week and then the dinner shift the next week. At first I absolutely loved it because one week I would spend my days on the beach and the next I would spend my evenings investigating the local nightlife. I had the best of both worlds. The only problem was that they kept on increasing my workload, and eventually I was feeling totally stressed and overworked. Then they wanted to promote me to full-time. Of course this would have involved a pay raise, but full-time workers had to work overtime as well. And I felt that if I was always working I wouldn't be able to enjoy the experience of living in a foreign country. When I refused the promotion my boss got really angry and decided to actually demote me! In the end I just gave up and handed in my notice. I felt like it was time to move to another country anyway.

Vocabulary and Phrases:

(To work) part-time/a part-time job: This is a job that is not full-time.

Example 1: *I spend most of my time writing books so I can only work part-time in another job.*

Example 2: *When I was at university I got a part-time job in a bar.*

Shift work: This is a job where the working hours are not just nine to five. Maybe there is a night shift, a morning shift and an evening shift. Often employees change what shift they work throughout the month. This means that someone doesn't always have to do the night shift. All the employees share the responsibility.

Example: *When I was younger I used to do shift work. But after I had kids I found it all too disruptive so I got a regular job.*

Workload: This refers to the actual work that you do. It also refers to how much work you are expected to do.

Example: *Ever since the recession started my workload has gone down. This is bad because I end up making less money.*

To be overworked: This is when you are working too much. You are given too much to do and it is affecting you badly.

Example: *His staff are completely overworked. It's crazy really, because they'll all just end up quitting.*

A promotion: This is when you get a better job within the same company.

Example 1: *I finally got a promotion. It's more money but it's also more responsibility.*

Example 2: *After five years of really working hard at that company I finally got promoted.*

To get a raise: This is when your wage goes up. You get paid more money.

Example: *I got a raise at work but I also have to do more work now.*

Overtime: This is when you work over your agreed work hours. For example if you usually work 8 hours a day and then one day you have to work for 10 hours, then that is 2 hours overtime.

Note: This is paid work. If you don't get paid then it is 'unpaid overtime'

Example: *I usually only work 2 or 3 hours overtime a week.*

Demotion: This is when you get a worse job within the same company. It usually happens if you have done something wrong.

Example: *After I lost the company all of that money I was demoted. It was all too embarrassing so I eventually quit.*

To hand in your notice: To tell your employer that you no longer want to work there. You usually have to tell them a month (or 2 months etc) before you wish to leave.

Example: *When I handed in my notice my boss was pretty upset. He said that he wanted me to stay for at least a year longer. Unfortunately I want to move town so that would be impossible.*

Over the years I had all sorts of interesting jobs but I think the best paid one was when I got an appointment as an international liaison in a small town in Korea. It was a great job while it lasted but because of a problem with my visa they eventually had to give the post to a permanent resident. Because the whole thing was not my fault they decided to make me redundant rather than fire me. This meant that I received some extra money. Because I liked everyone there, on my last payday I used some of my redundancy money to take everyone from my office out to dinner.

Vocabulary and Phrases:

An appointment: This refers to when someone gets a job. It is often for quite a good job.

Example: *He was appointed as the managing director early last year.*

A post: This refers to a job. A position.

Example: *I got the post as a headmaster after working at that school for over 10 years.*

To be made redundant: This is when you lose your job but it is not your fault. Perhaps the company is not doing very well and they no longer have enough money to employ you.

Example 1: *After 20 years of working at the same company my father was made redundant.*

Example 2: *The good thing about being made redundant is that you get redundancy pay.*

To be fired: This is when you lose your job due to a bad reason. Your employers say that they don't want you to work there anymore.

Example: *My son is always getting fired from jobs. He's just got such a bad attitude.*

Payday: This is the day of the week/month that you get paid.

Example: *I go out with my work colleagues every payday.*

I think that the most unusual job that I did while traveling was to work on a magazine in the USA. The problem was that the magazine was running out of money so there were no permanent offices. This meant that all of the staff had to hot desk and then communicate with each other via email and phone. Also most of the employees were working flexi-time so it was impossible to get anyone on the phone. Of course the whole thing was a mess and it went bankrupt a few months after I started there. When I think back through my career, I may not have made a lot of money, but I've definitely had a lot of different occupations!

Vocabulary and Phrases:

Hot desking: This refers to when you hire a desk to work from. You don't have an office, just a desk in someone else's office.

Example: *I hot desked for about a year, but got annoyed with always having to clear up everything at the end of the day. Eventually I just hired an office and it actually saves me a lot of time nowadays.*

Flexi-time: This is when an employee has to work a certain amount of hours a week but they can do it any time that they like. It doesn't matter when they work as long as they work the full amount of hours that is expected of them.

Example 1: *I don't really like flexi-time. I prefer the structure of a nine to five job.*

Example 2: *I work flexi-time. So I have to work 10 hours a week but it doesn't matter when I do it. I tend to try to do most of the work on Monday and Tuesday so that I don't have to worry about it later in the week.*

An occupation: This is what your job is. If you are a teacher then your occupation is 'teaching'.

Example: *I didn't know what occupation I wanted when I left school so I decided to go traveling first.*

Marriage

Part One

I have twin uncles. The thing is that while they look identical, they actually have completely different personalities. They basically don't agree on anything, especially on the matter of 'matrimony'.

My uncle Bill has basically been a bachelor most of his life. He eventually met a woman and fell in love but still refuses to get married. He is now in something he calls a 'civil partnership'. This is where they live as 'husband and wife' but they are not actually married. When I asked him why he didn't tie the knot he just mumbled that 'love, fidelity and respect' was all he needed, not a marriage certificate. I personally think that he's so against marriage because his twin brother seems to get married every couple of weeks! And he'd hate to be like his brother in any way.

Vocabulary and Phrases:

Matrimony: This refers to marriage.

Example: *You should never enter into matrimony lightly. You need to be sure that this is the person that you want to spend your whole life with.*

Bachelor: This is an unmarried man. It often means that he is not in a relationship at all. He is single.

Example: *My best friend has always been a bachelor, he's never been interested in marriage.*

A civil partnership: This is when a couple lives like a married couple but they are not actually married.

Example: *They were in a civil partnership so when he died she automatically inherited everything.*

To tie the knot: This is a casual phrase which means 'to get married'.

Example: *Me and my partner decided to finally tie the knot after being together for nearly 10 years.*

Fidelity: This means that you don't cheat on your partner. You do not have affairs. The opposite of 'fidelity' is 'infidelity'.

Example 1: *Fidelity is essential for a long happy marriage.*

Example 2: *I was pretty shocked to hear that infidelity is becoming more and more common.*

A marriage certificate: This is the official document you get to prove that you are actually married.

Example: *When we decided to emigrate the embassy insisted on seeing our marriage certificate.*

My other uncle Tim, is the complete opposite of Bill. In fact he has been married 4 times. His first marriage only lasted 2 weeks! My mother told me that it was due to 'adultery', which is pretty shocking considering that they were on honeymoon for most of their marriage. Of course uncle Tim completely denies this and says that he never wanted to get married to her in the first place. He told me that "it was a shotgun wedding, neither of us wanted to get married but her family insisted once she got pregnant". I'm pretty sure that this is absolute nonsense as he's never had kids! I think he just makes up stories because he is embarrassed that me cheated on his spouse after only a few weeks.

Vocabulary and Phrases:

Adultery: This is when the husband or wife has a sexual partner other than their spouse. They cheat on their husband/wife.

Example: *Adultery almost always ends up ruining a marriage in one way or another.*

A honeymoon: This is the holiday just after a couple gets married.

Example: *We spent our honeymoon in the West Indies.*

A shotgun wedding: This is when an unmarried couple gets pregnant and then immediately decides to get married.

Example: *They suddenly got married so most people just think that it must be a shotgun wedding.*

A spouse: This refers to your husband or wife. If you are married then the other person is your spouse.

Example: *I met my spouse at work. We started dating and then after a year or so we got married.*

After his first marriage he started a business and became quite wealthy. So the next time he got engaged everyone told him that he must get a 'pre-nup' before getting married. Of course he just ignored everyone and eventually that marriage ended in divorce and a huge divorce settlement. After that, he had hardly any money left so he agreed to a 'marriage of convenience' to make a little extra cash. Luckily they didn't have a ceremony with the bride and groom making vows and stuff. Everyone knew the marriage was fake and just so she could get a visa. His current and hopefully last marriage seems to be genuine and hopefully it will last.

Vocabulary and Phrases:

An engagement: If you 'get engaged' then that means that you have agreed to get married to someone. The 'engagement' is the period from the proposal to the actual wedding.

Example 1: *My parents met when they were at school and then got engaged as soon as they were 18 years old.*

Example 2: *It's more and more common to have quite long engagements nowadays.*

Pre-nup: This refers to a 'pre-nuptial agreement'. This is a legal agreement people sometimes make before they get married. This says exactly how much money etc each party will get if the marriage ends in a divorce.

Example: *Luckily she got a pre-nup, otherwise she would have ended up losing half of her money.*

Divorce settlement: If you get divorced you may have to divide your assets up. This is called a divorce settlement.

Example: *I heard that she did a lot better than him on the divorce settlement.*

A marriage of convenience: This is when people get married not for love but for other reasons. The main reason is when someone wants to stay in a certain country so they get married for a visa. This is an arrangement between the two parties. It is often illegal and especially not allowed when it is done for visa reasons.

Example: *She wanted to stay in the country so she got married. It was a marriage of convenience and she had to pay the guy quite a lot of money.*

Bride: This is the lady that is getting married.

Example: *The bride looks amazing in that dress.*

Groom: This is the man that is getting married.

Example: *The groom is starting to look a little worried! Perhaps he's having second thoughts.*

Wedding vows: Often when people get married they say their 'vows' to each other during the wedding ceremony. These vows are like promises to each other that they will keep during their marriage.

Example: *The thing about wedding vows is that most people never actually keep them.*

MORE USEFUL WORDS:

Monogamy: This is when you only have one sexual partner at a time. You do not cheat on your partner.

Example: *Most married couples believe in monogamy.*

A marriage proposal: This is when someone asks someone else to marry them.

Example: *I proposed to my wife after only a month of knowing her.*

To ask for someone's hand in marriage: To ask someone to marry you.

Example: *In some cultures it is polite to ask the parents of the woman for permission before you ask for their daughter's hand in marriage.*

Marriage/Wedding Youtube Channels:

Modern Wedding.

Brides.

POLITICS

PART ONE

Sam Hawthorn has had what can only be described as an 'unusual and eventful political career'. He came from what he describes as a normal working class, but definitely non-partisan family. He never had much interest in politics and defiantly never dreamed that he would become a politician in the future. He left school at 18 and started working in a local factory. He was immediately struck by the bad conditions he and his colleagues were working in. This experience made him become an activist. He soon started a grassroots movement which lobbied the government to introduce much stricter employment laws that protected workers' rights. The new reforms were so popular that Sam was often in the media spotlight.

Vocabulary and Phrases:

Partisan: This is someone/an idea that firmly supports a certain political party/ideology.

Example: *Even though I work for that political party, I try not to be partisan in my private life. I have friends who have different political beliefs from mine.*

An activist: This is someone (not a politician) who takes action to push a certain political/social idea.

Example: *Lots of green activists are targeting cattle farmers as one of the main causes of global warming.*

Grassroots (movement): This is when a group of people (not politicians) start pushing a certain political idea. For example if people start campaigning against the building of power stations in their area, then that is a 'grassroots campaign'.

Example: *What started as a grassroots movement has now gone mainstream. Now even some politicians are against the planned changes to pensions.*

To lobby/a lobby group/a lobbyist: To try to influence political thinking/ a group that tries to influence political policies/ a person who tries to influence political policies.

Example 1: *The tobacco industry has been trying to lobby the government to loosen the laws around health warnings.*

Example 2: *That lobby group tries to influence policy in favor of the pharmaceutical industry.*

Example 3: *I find it hard to trust lobbyists. Do they actually believe in the policies they are trying to push? Or are they just doing it because it's their job?*

Reforms: These are changes to policies and laws. Usually meant to make things better and more up to date.

Example: *The prison reforms are expected to be agreed upon next week.*

Because he had become so famous as a grassroots activist, he was soon asked to join the main opposition party. He agreed and campaigned to become a member of parliament*. His political ideology was definitely left-wing and he campaigned on a platform of fairer conditions for workers. He was going against a pretty popular candidate from the ruling party, but due to his strong message the polls showed that he was definitely going to win. The polls were right and he won by a landslide.

*This is the job title of a UK politician.

Vocabulary and Phrases:

The opposition (party): This is the political party that is not in power. Not the ruling party.

Example: *The opposition are very against this new policy, even though it was actually originally their idea when they were in power last year.*

A (political) campaign: This is when a politician tries to get elected. They run a campaign to show voters that they should vote for them.

Example: *He ran a pretty good campaign. But in the end the other candidate was just more popular.*

Ideology: A set of ideas and values.

Example: *I don't like that party's ideology. They don't seem to care about poorer people at all.*

Left/right-wing: This describes ones political ideas. Left-wing is often towards 'society' and rightwing is often towards 'individuals'.

Example: *I was quite right-wing when I was younger but I've become more and more left-wing over the years.*

A platform (of): This describes what a politician/political party say they are going to do if they get elected.

Example: *He was voted in on his very 'ecological' platform. But he's actually done nothing to help the environment since he got into power.*

A candidate: This is a politician who is hoping to be voted into office. They hope to be voted into power.

Example: *The presidential candidate has been campaigning for months now.*

The ruling party/governing party: This is the political party that is in power. The government.

Example: *I can't tell the difference between the ruling and the opposition parties anymore.*

A poll: This is a type of vote. It is often used to check what the public opinion is on a certain matter.

Example: *The government conducted a poll to see if people would be in favor of changing the health system.*

A landslide (victory): This is when someone/a political party wins by a large amount.

Example: *The opposition party won by a landslide. So it looks like we will have a new government as of tomorrow.*

As you know most politicians tend to break their promises as soon as they get elected. They also tend to mellow in their ideas somewhat. But Sam was the complete opposite, actually his views got stronger the longer he was in politics. He remained a 'straight talker' throughout his career. In fact it was this complete lack of 'spin' that gained him popularity with the general public but not with his fellow politicians. He was constantly upsetting both his own and the other political parties. His career ended when he pretty much destroyed all the alliances that he had by suggesting that the incumbent Prime Minister should be impeached. As you can imagine this was not a popular opinion and he was basically fired on the spot. Although his time as a politician was short, it certainly was entertaining to watch.

Vocabulary and Phrases:

Spin/spin doctor: 'Spin' describes changing how people view a certain policy. Manipulating public opinion. A 'spin doctor' tries to present a policy in a way that the public would agree to it.

Example 1: *I don't listen to politicians anymore. It's all just spin. They never just tell the straight truth.*

Example 2: *There are too many spin doctors in politics. It's all about making bad policies look good.*

An alliance: This is when two people/parties join together to achieve something.

Example: *The alliance between the two parties over health care reforms will probably not last too long.*

The incumbent (President etc): This is the President/Prime Minister that is currently in power.

Example: *The incumbent president will have to fight very hard to win this election.*

Impeachment: This is when the head of state (President/Prime minister etc) is fired. They are forced to quit.

Example: *Was Nixon the last president to be impeached?*

News Youtube channels that feature some discussion of politics:

Channel 4 News.

CNN

BBC News

STARTING A BUSINESS

PART ONE

I bumped into an old school friend of mine the other day. We hadn't seen each other in years so it was interesting to catch up. When I told her that I was an entrepreneur she said that she wasn't surprised and that I was always a bit of a 'risk taker'. That got me thinking about start-ups; are they that risky? Of course at the beginning it can all be a bit worrying. I mean, even if you have a little seed money, cash flow can be a be a problem. Especially if you don't have much money coming in yet. But I think that if you are careful then starting a business doesn't actually have to be that risky.

Vocabulary and Phrases:

An entrepreneur: This is someone who starts up a new company.

Example: *The thing about being an entrepreneur that I don't like is that it can be a bit lonely.*

(To be) a risk taker: This phrase is often used about entrepreneurs. Of course it just describes someone who takes risks.

Example: *If you are going to be a risk taker you need to be prepared to fail occasionally.*

A start-up: This phrase refers to a new business enterprise.

Example: *A lot of new start-ups are online businesses.*

Seed money: This is money for starting a new business.

Example: *I used up most of my seed money in the first 6 months of starting my business. Luckily I had money coming in by that point.*

Cash-flow: This refers to the money coming in and going out of a business. What you earn *vs* what you spend on the business.

Example: *When you are starting out, make sure that you pay attention to cash flow or you could run into some serious problems.*

PART TWO

Here are some hints so you don't have to take too many risks when starting a new business.

One) Make sure that you choose a niche where people actually buy things. That way you know there will be customers waiting to buy your products.

Two) Make sure that you write a detailed business plan. That way you will have less surprises along the way.

Three) Do some 'test sales' or 'test trading'. That way you can be sure the product will be popular before you buy in lots of stock.

Four) If you are not sure about a product, try 'drop shipping'. That way the manufacturer rather than you takes the risk.

Five) If your business is not going well and you are thinking of quitting, try pivoting instead. You may just need to change direction a bit rather than stopping altogether.

Of course there are other things you should do to avoid risk but these five points are the ones that helped me the most.

Vocabulary and Phrases:

Niche: a small specialized area/subject.

Example: *I have a very niche business, so there isn't too much competition.*

A business plan: A detailed written plan about how you are going to start and build your business.

Example: *Banks usually want to see your business plan before they will lend you any money.*

(To do) test trading: This is when you try to sell a few items to see if they are popular. If they are, then you buy in stock and start selling seriously.

Example: *Luckily I did some test trading, because it turns out that the item is not popular at all.*

Drop shipping: This is when you sell an item (usually through a website) and then it is sent directly to the customer from the manufacturer. This saves you from keeping any stock.

Example: *You may make less profit doing drop shipping, but you also have less risk.*

Pivoting: This is when you slightly change the direction of your business if things are not going that well. Instead of just quitting you change the direction.

Example: *Luckily I pivoted my business and now it's pretty successful.*

Extra Practice.

Business Start-up Youtube channels:

This Week in Start-Ups.

Abdul Mohhamed. This person often speaks about business and uses a lot of useful language.

TRAVELING

When I was younger my parents absolutely refused to ever spend any money. All of my clothes were second hand and we didn't even have a TV until I was about 16. I always found it embarrassing at school as I was the only one who didn't get any pocket money. The only thing my parents would spend money on was going away on holidays abroad or on short getaways to the country. My mother used to say that travel was the best type of education there was, and that you'd learn things that you never would in a classroom. Mostly we did cheap holidays and never had a package holiday. Often we would just drive around Europe on a whistle-stop tour of all the 'educational' spots that my mother had marked on our itinerary. Usually we would camp or stay in a hostel and if we were really lucky we got to stay in a half board hotel. When I got older I didn't want to go traveling anymore and had no interest in backpacking around the world with my friends. I felt that I'd already done enough travelling and usually just did a staycation over the summer holidays instead.

Vocabulary and Phrases:

(A short) getaway: This describes a very short holiday.

Example: *I rarely get the chance to go abroad nowadays. Usually I just have a quick getaway with my wife somewhere close.*

A package holiday: This is a holiday where the flight, hotel and sometimes the meals are included in the price.

Example: *I love going on package holidays. Everything is taken care of, there is nothing else to worry about.*

A whistle-stop tour: This is when you travel around and stop at places for a very short time. You do not stay in one area/town for long.

Example: *Next year I'm going to do a 10 day whistle-stop tour of Asia. In total I will visit 5 countries.*

An itinerary: This is a list of things to do. A schedule.

Example: *When I travel for business there is usually a strict itinerary so I rarely get a chance to do any sightseeing.*

A hostel: This is like a hotel but it is cheaper and more basic. Sometimes you have to share a room with other people.

Example: *Staying in hostels is an excellent and cheap way to travel around England.*

Half board/full board: 'Half board' in a hotel is when you get a room and breakfast, but no dinner. 'Full board' is when you get a room and all of your meals (sometimes not lunch) included.

Example: *I think that the holiday is £300 half board or £500 full board.*

Backpacking: This is when you travel around carrying everything in a backpack. Usually you don't use a car. Often you camp or stay in cheap accommodation such as a hostel.

Example: *When I was 18 I backpacked around Australia.*

A staycation: This is a 'new' word and is when you stay in your own country on holiday. You don't go abroad on *va*cation.

Example: *Recently staycations have become more and more popular. Less people have the money to go abroad anymore.*

Travel Youtube channels:

Wunderlusts.

In Transit.

EXERCISE

PART ONE

Until the age of 30 I never had to worry about my weight or fitness. I was one of those annoying people who just stayed naturally slim without counting calories. Also because I was always pretty active I managed to stay looking toned without doing any real exercise. Anyway for some reason at the age of 30 I suddenly became really overweight. Because I'd never had to worry about that stuff before I realized that I knew nothing about getting in shape and that I'd have to learn everything from the beginning.

Vocabulary and Phrases:

To calorie count: This is when you check how many calories each piece of food you eat contains. To not eat too many calories.

Example: *I don't believe in calorie counting. I think that you should just try to eat healthily.*

To be toned: To have firm muscles.

Example: *Doing Pilates makes your whole body look toned.*

To get in shape: To become fit.

Example: *I want to get in shape before the summer.*

I was determined to shed the pounds so I read every health and fitness book I could find. Most of them recommended calorie restricting but I knew that I would never last on a diet. In the end I decided to just eat as healthily as possible and to work out in the gym 4 times a week. As I knew nothing about exercise, I joined a few classes in the gym. This was great because they tell you exactly what to do; when to inhale/exhale during the exercises, how to warm up etc. I particularly liked the classes where you could exert yourself and work up a good sweat. I found that with cardio you tend to enter the fat burning zone after 30 minutes. So the better your endurance is, the more weight you will lose. After about six months I also noticed that if I stayed properly hydrated, my recovery times would be a lot shorter. It's a funny thing but getting fat was actually a good thing because it forced me to learn about health and fitness and how to look after my body.

Vocabulary and Phrases:

To shed the pounds: To lose weight.

Example: *The easiest way that I have found to shed the pounds quickly, is to jump rope. It's amazingly effective.*

Calorie restriction: This is when you cut down on the calories you consume.

Example: *I find that calorie restriction never works long term. You should just try to be consistent and eat more healthily.*

To work out/a work out: To do a session of physical exercise.

Example 1: *I try to work out every morning.*

Example 2: *I had a pretty exhausting workout this morning.*

To inhale/exhale: To breathe in/out.

Example: *When doing yoga it is important to inhale and exhale at the right moments.*

To warm-up: To slowly get ready for exercise. To ease into exercise.

Example: *It's important to warm-up before you go for a run.*

To exert yourself: To fully use your energy.

Example: *When exercising you should try to not over-exert yourself.*

To work up a sweat: To exercise to the point that you are sweating.

Example: *Jogging is a good way to really work up a sweat.*

To do cardio: 'Cardio' refers to 'cardiovascular exercise' and means when you do exercise that works your lungs and gets your blood pumping more quickly. For example running, jump rope etc.

Example: *I much prefer cardio to weight training.*

The fat burning zone: This is the point during exercise where the body really starts to burn off fat.

Example: *I always try to exercise hard enough so that I enter the fat burning zone.*

Endurance: The ability to keep going.

Example: *Once you build up your endurance while jogging, you can pretty much just keep going for hours.*

To be hydrated: To have enough water in your body. To keep drinking enough.

Example: *If you feel tired during the day it could be because you are not hydrated enough.*

Recovery time: This is how long it takes you to recover from exercise.

Example: *Once I started to eat more fruit my recovery time got a lot shorter.*

Exercise Youtube Channels:

Befit.

Blogilates.

Six Pack Shortcut.

Fazit

Well done and thanks for reading.

Denken Sie daran: Wenn Sie weitermachen, jeden Tag ein bisschen, dann erreichen Sie Ihr Ziel des flüssigen Sprechens.

Wenn Ihnen dieses Buch gefallen hat und Sie der Meinung sind, dass es auch für andere hilfreich sein könnte, dann nehmen Sie sich bitte einen Augenblick Zeit und schreiben Sie eine Bewertung. Kleinverleger wie ich können ihre Bücher nicht wie die größeren Unternehmen vermarkten, deshalb sind wir stark von Bewertungen abhängig, um das Buch bekannt zu machen.

Wenn Sie Spaß daran hatten, dieses Buch zu lesen, dann denke ich, dass Sie sich auch 500 Wirklich Nützliche Englische Sätze. ansehen sollten, da es den selben Schwierigkeitsgrad besitzt und perfekt ist, wenn Sie natürliches, alltägliches Englisch lernen möchten und zwar auf einfache Art, die auch noch Spaß macht.

Wenn Sie sich gerne für meinen Newsletter registrieren möchten, um kostenlose Lernmaterialien zu erhalten, besuchen Sie bitte meine Website.

englishfluencytoday.com/de/kostenloses-horverstehen-mp3.html

Good luck on your journey to English fluency.